The Healthy High Performance Way

A Practical Guide to Developing Mindful Habits That Revitalise Your Performance Mindset and Boost Accomplishment

L A Worley

Business Brilliance Professional Development Ltd

Published 2023 by Business Brilliance Professional Development Ltd

A catalogue record for this book is available from the British Library.

Cover Design: akira007/akiragraphicz
ISBN: 978-1-7393901-0-5

Contents

Foreword

Since publishing my first book *Just Notice* in December 2020, the focus of my practice has expanded. Clients have come with performance issues that encompass areas of life other than the workplace.

In fact, many of my clients have been young people who struggled with performance challenges in areas such as friendships, academics and self-care. As a result, I have expanded the focus and changed the title to address performance issues, making it relevant to a wider community of people.

Bringing mindfulness to my own practice, I recognised what it is that I do that makes my work so impactful. I have created a neural pathway re-engineering framework called I-AM-I, which I share in this book for the first time.

Given the current state of the world in which we're living, I know that people need to practise the art of mindfulness now more than ever. Old structures are breaking down and new ones are being built in a whole range of areas including government, finance, healthcare and so on.

This is good! It needs to happen. We have to break down old processes that no longer work to make way for new ones to develop. Re-engineering your neural pathways to create performance efficiency works on the same principle.

It's tempting to want everyone else to change. However, the one person for whom you are responsible is you. While change can be daunting, it is also liberating. The more committed we are to living from truth and peace rather than competition and fear, the better able we'll be to create a world that works for EVERYONE.

According to Mahatma Gandhi, "If we could change ourselves, the tendencies in the world would also change." And Oscar Wilde famously said, "Be yourself: everyone else is already taken."

That's what this book is designed to do — to help you develop self-awareness through the practical application of mindfulness and use it to practise self-governance, which fuels high performance and elevates self-mastery. Applying mindfulness makes self-mastery feel as natural as breathing when you do it, one breath at a time. I look forward to showing you how.

Chapter 1

Why This Book on Mindfulness?

There are a lot of books on mindfulness, just as there are a lot of books on high performance. Why should you choose this one? How is it different?

For a start, I want to make mindfulness simple, relevant and accessible. Working in the field of personal development and mental well-being since the late 1990s, I've seen well-meaning practitioners unintentionally diminish mindfulness's potential. I want to show you what's possible when you learn how to apply it to something practical like performance.

In recent years, many of my clients have come to me with specific performance issues in various life situations. While their challenges may be different, they all share a similar combination of feelings: regret and powerlessness at their inability to perform in a particular area of life, combined with anxiety when faced with a situation where they will be required to perform again. They feel frustrated because they tend to be high performers, meaning they derive pleasure from performing at a high level.

They have reached what I call a performance plateau. Their normal strategies have stopped working, and they are looking for ways to free themselves from their flattened performance so they can reach performance peaks again.

I have written this book with the intention of it being a discovery for you, whether you consider yourself to be a high performer or not. I want you to finish this book with a felt, embodied sense of what mindfulness is and what it makes possible for you.

I intend to show you just how valuable mindfulness really is to your ability to achieve performance goals in a healthy way in many areas of life, including academics, career, love, relationships, health, well-being, even spirituality.

I've made it practical because I know that experience, combined with knowledge and the capacity to fully observe the experience, is the best teacher you have.

This book is designed to engage your own capacity to think, feel and experience your relationship to performance and the relevance that mindfulness brings to your participation in life as an empowered, active, engaged human being. Treating you as a passive, dormant lump won't help you achieve that objective, and it won't help me share the performance enhancements you can obtain by practising mindfulness in an embodied way.

A great way for you to get the best out of this book is to choose a goal that's important for you to fulfil. Create that as the context for the questions and exercises through which I guide you.

In fact, imagine me as your coach, and we are having a discussion about your goals. I ask questions, the purpose of which is to help you find the answers that are most meaningful to you. Not me. YOU!

Some of the questions might make sense. Others may be completely foreign to you. And some might seem simply irrelevant. That's OK. Trust yourself to take what you need and leave the rest.

As your participation continues, I want you to appreciate the opportunity to know yourself as a high-performing person rather than observing it from a distance as a nice idea. I want you to be so taken with the benefits mindfulness brings to your performance in life that you choose to explore the path even further. I want you to discover how it will empower you to master your participation in life.

If you are a working person, you spend a lot of time at the workplace. It is the perfect environment in which to explore the effects mindfulness brings to your performance. It will expand your ability to know your value and make a valuable contribution to your workplace ecosystem.

If you're a student, a stay-at-home parent, a carer, a retiree or a person of leisure, this book can help you, too. Choose an area of your life where you'd like to up your game. It could be improving your backhand or your tee shot. It could be learning to manage your anxiety around exams. It could be remaining calm and present when you're with your family.

These are all useful things to take away from this experience, aren't they?

For the remainder of the book, allow me to be your guide. Chart your discoveries and your performance improvements along the way. Incorporate these practices into your daily routine. Learn to observe yourself in a way you may have never done so before.

As you hone your observational skills, witness what happens. You are in for some surprises.

This is going to be fun and easier than you think, I promise. Let's get started.

Chapter 2

What Is Performance?

What is the most efficient way of improving your performance? And can you achieve an increase in performance with less work?

It's an age-old quest humankind has sought to solve since the discovery of the wheel. Invention after invention serves to help us achieve more with less – more speed with less power, more efficiency with less time, and so on.

You may demand this of yourself at home, work or school. Perhaps other people demand this of you. If you are committed to high performance, it's likely you search for the right tools and create structures and processes to support your performance enhancement goals.

While searching for tried and tested strategies certainly helps, consider that you have omitted a key part of the equation – you. Consider that looking outside yourself for the answers only solves part of the problem.

To address performance with integrity, you need to turn your attention within, too. Observe yourself in action. Relate to yourself in the same way you relate to other people. Make decisions based on both intrinsic and extrinsic information

Why? It provides you with the power to activate the Witness, the part of you that is capable of taking a bird's eye view of any situation. By activating and utilising the Witness, you discover ways of doing things you would not have seen otherwise.

You stop being a victim of circumstance and you become an agent of transformation. You manage hurdles with increasing ease. You catch potential obstacles before they turn into major issues.

In short, you enter the realm of being a responsible person who creates opportunity and makes a contribution in the process. You exercise your true creative potential.

You step into your power, and life starts to flow with a new sense of ease.

Interested? Keep reading.

You might be wondering how I know this.

I began my foray into the world of mindfulness at a young age, nine, in fact. Watching a Tina Turner interview, I discovered she turned to meditation to help her heal from the domestic abuse she experienced as Ike's wife. It piqued my curiosity.

So, I set off to my bedroom, chanting in an attempt to reach the state of peace and expanded awareness she described. Nothing happened.

A few years later, I was introduced to mindful breathing during a typing class in high school. The exercise, combining the imagery of a cloud entering and leaving my chest with the flow of my breath in and out, made a noticeable impact on my state of mind. I often turned to it at moments when I wanted to restore calm.

When I took up yoga as a practice in the late 1990s after my first trip to India, I discovered the benefits of combining visualisation, the breath and movement to my overall sense of well-being. By this time, I was convinced of the benefits of mindfulness.

During my training as an integrative psychotherapist, I was instantly drawn to body-centred mindfulness as a key part of my work with clients. The body holds a record of all our experiences. If you want to free yourself from hidden constraints and expand your performance - and your awareness with it - the fastest and most effective way to do

7

it is to work with the mind and the body as an integrated whole.

These days, I help people expand their performance in lots of areas, including business, sports, academics, relationships and leadership.

The challenges are surprisingly similar, and the use of the breath is a fundamental element of expanding performance. It helps you connect to deeper parts of yourself and expand intrinsic motivation. We'll dive deeper into that a little later.

The beauty of the breath is that it accompanies you wherever you go. It's a wonderful tool to help you experience a deeper side of life. Experiment with it. Value it. And value yourself in the process.

Before we begin, I want to let you know that there are contraindications to breath work. What does that mean? If you have certain conditions or symptoms, you should avoid engaging in it.

Why? Because breath work can release physical, emotional and psychological energy that may produce unexpected and intense experiences.

While the exercises I teach you in this book are gentle, your health is my top priority. If you have any doubts, please do not practice mindfulness without the face-to-face guidance of a professional.

There are both physical and mental health contraindications, so please be responsible for your health by taking the recommendations seriously. I have taken these contraindications from Breathwork Online. [1]

For your benefit, here's the list:

Medical Contraindications

- Epilepsy
- Detached Retina
- Glaucoma
- Osteoporosis that is serious enough, whereby moving around actively could cause potential issues
- High Blood Pressure that is not controlled with medication
- Cardiovascular disease and/or irregularities, including prior heart attack
- Strokes, seizures, TIAs or other brain/neurological conditions or disease
- If either you have had an aneurysm or if two members of your immediate family have had one
- Use of prescription blood thinning medications such as Coumadin
- Pregnancy
- Asthma (if you have asthma, you can participate but you must have your inhaler available)

Psychiatric Contraindications

- Prior diagnosis by a health professional of bipolar disorder or schizophrenia
- Hospitalisation for any psychiatric condition or emotional crisis during the past 10 years
- PTSD with strong symptoms (seek the guidance of a mental health professional before participating)
- Any other medical, psychiatric or physical conditions which would impair or affect the ability to engage in any activities that involve intense physical and/or emotional release.

How To Use This Book

Let me address something before we go further.

I know it may seem strange to start reading a book and immediately be faced with a whole series of questions. Most reading experiences are passive. Usually, you read books to get answers, don't you?

I'd argue it depends on the type of books you read!

Here's how I recommend you use this book. Read it all the way through the first time around. You'll get the gist of it. Then, start from the beginning and read it one chapter at a time, giving yourself a week or so to digest the contents of each chapter.

Buy yourself a lovely journal and record your answers to the questions and your experiences of the exercises. If you wish, you can pick up a copy of the workbook journal I've created to accompany the book. It makes it easy for you to keep track of your discoveries and your results in an organised way.

Why is recording your discoveries important? Writing down your thoughts grounds them onto the page. Rather than continuing to swirl in your head like a whisper, your thoughts become manifestations on a page when you record them. This creates distance between you and your thoughts, enabling you to witness them with greater objectivity than you can when they remain elusively ethereal.

I also recommend that you use pen and paper rather than an electronic device to record your thoughts. Firstly, writing gives you greater connection to your thoughts as objects of your creation. Secondly, your handwriting is a unique expression of you. If you choose to type them at a later date, that's fine. In the first instance, though, allow yourself to connect to the act of writing.

Maybe you could bring mindfulness to the action of using pen and paper. What might you discover?

There's your first opportunity to get mindful! Write down what arises as you consider the conversation about writing.

Let's continue. Ask yourself: 'What does performance mean to me?'

As you're contemplating the idea of performance, grab your journal and jot down what performance means to you.

Not to a dictionary, but to *you*.

You may be tempted to do an internet search. I'm not looking for you to demonstrate that you know the right answer. I want you to look at your life and discover *your* actual relationship to performance.

(By the way, there is no right answer.)

Why am I asking you to do this?

There are loads of potential reasons why, but the fundamental one is this: I want you to be aware of what your relationship to performance actually is, right now, in this moment.

Human beings, especially those of us who have been educated in a school system, have been trained to fit our thinking into pre-defined boxes. Let's see if you can shake off that method of learning for a moment.

I promise we will look into the pre-defined boxes and examine the contents. For now, I invite you to begin this exploration by revealing to yourself what you already know about the box I'm calling performance.

Deal?

Performance Considerations

Let's examine your relationship to performance in a little more detail. Here are some questions to answer, recording your answers in your journal.

What do you experience when you hear the word 'performance'? In particular, what do you:

- See?
- Hear?
- Remember?
- Feel?
- Sense?
- Smell?
- Taste?

Using the experiential guide in the previous question, consider what arises when you think of performance in the following areas:

- Family
- Friendship
- Academics
- Career
- Workplace
- Finances
- Romance

- Health
- Social.

How do your performance capabilities impact:

- You?
- Your family?
- Your friends?
- Your colleagues?
- Your career?
- Your opportunities?
- Your future?

By the way, the bullet points are designed to offer you suggestions of places you could look. However, do not be limited by them. If something is pressing and it's not on the list, please add it. Equally, if a suggestion is irrelevant, skip over it.

Remember: this is your experience. This is your discovery. I am acting as a guide who will recommend you cast your gaze in particular directions, AND I actively encourage you to veer off the path into the wilderness. It's about what is appropriate for you.

The Definition of Performance

We began this chapter by asking the question, "What is performance?" Now that you've had a chance to consider your own relationship with performance, we will consult the experts to find out how performance is defined.

Before we get into the definition, I want to draw your attention to a particular facet of this book. You'll notice that throughout the book, I use a couple of dictionaries. I choose a variety of sources because I am looking for the simplest and most complete definitions, and these can vary from source to source.

I also like to acknowledge as many extraordinary sources as possible. It gives me a feel-good boost to know I am sharing the love.

It's important to mention why I share definitions and the etymology of words with you. Firstly, sharing the definition of a word brings clarity, giving us a clear framework for our discussion. Secondly, knowing the etymology of a word gives us a greater understanding of the origins and the DNA of a word. To create change that endures, it's best to go to the source. The reasons for this will become obvious as the book and the discovery unfolds.

Let's look at the pre-defined box called 'performance.' The Cambridge English Dictionary defines performance as:

- How well a person, machine, etc does a piece of work or activity

- The action of entertaining other people by dancing, singing, acting or playing music
- The act of doing something, such as your job
- Performance also refers to how well an activity or job is done
- How successful an investment, company, etc is and how much profit it makes
- How well a computer, machine, etc works
- How well someone does their job or duties
- The act of doing what is stated in a legal agreement.[2]

As you read through the definition, notice what arises for you. Has your attitude to performance changed? Does something about the definition jump out at you? Can you identify a common theme in the definitions?

It could be helpful at this stage to revisit the questions with the bullet points I posed earlier. They will help you reflect upon and apply performance as a concept to various aspects of your life. Record what you notice in your journal.

Now, let's dive a little deeper and look at the etymology, or the origin, of the word 'performance'.

The infinitive *to perform* originated in the 13th century as a derivation of the Old French word *parfornir*, meaning 'to do, carry out, finish, accomplish', from *par,* meaning 'completely' and *fornir,* meaning 'to provide'. Performance as a noun emerged in the 15th century, taking on the meaning 'accomplishment or completion'. [3]

When you look at performance's DNA, what do you notice?

For me, the words that stand out are 'completely', 'completion' and 'finish'. They suggest that, at its core, performance literally means to carry out something completely and to completion.

In life, these words are often loaded with significance. Let's think about it for a moment by considering the following questions. Write down what you notice in your journal.

- What does it mean to complete a task?
- What does it mean to fail to complete a task?
- What does it mean to perform well?
- What does it mean to perform poorly?
- How would you know?
- On a scale of one to 10, one being terrible, 10 being exemplary, how would you rate your performance in life?
- What evidence can you provide to support your rating?
- How do you feel about your rating?
- Where and how is the feeling expressing itself?

As you finish answering the questions, gently take a deep breath in through your nose and then release gently through the mouth. Do this three times.

Notice what's happening as you release the last deep breath. Record your experience in your journal.

Measuring Performance

In life, good performance can refer to a whole host of things - academic, sporting, health, business, team, departmental, project, initiative, equipment, technological, regional, cultural, financial, social, physical, artistic, societal, strategic, company and governmental performance.

This is a small sample of the areas of life in which performance is often assessed.

This, then, begs the question, "How is performance assessed?"

In academic settings, performance is measured through grades. In business, performance is tracked and assessed using KPIs, which stand for Key Performance Indicators. Health performance can be determined by things like body temperature, the level of oxygen in the breath and both the presence and the amount of certain substances in the bloodstream. In sports, performance is measured by speed, scores and stats like batting average. Cultural and societal performance is often determined by measurements such as average wage, unemployment figures and quality of life.

I think you've got the picture by now, right?

When you want to determine how well someone or something is performing, you measure it.

Let's take sports, for example. How do you know that a team is at the top of the league? A simple metric would be to keep a tally of the number of games the league teams win, lose and draw. The team with the largest number of wins and draws would be considered the best team in the league.

Now, I have oversimplified this analogy because the metrics are different for each sport, and in some cases, it gets rather complicated. Some are team sports, and some are individual sports, and in each case, the performance of individuals is important.

Why? The world of sport is big business. Understanding the performance of particular players helps the industry understand the benefits sportspeople bring to their team or their sport. This, in turn, determines whether or not a particular player is performing well enough to merit salaries, prize money, sporting accolades and lucrative sponsorship deals.

In sport, while personality certainly plays a significant role in a sportsperson's likability, most people are concerned with the performance on the court, pitch or course.

They want to back successful people. They celebrate winners.

How do you then derive meaning from the measurements? You compare individual measurements to metrics. In the case of sports again, the industry will take an average for a particular metric and then assess where a sportsperson's measurements lie on the statistical curve.

How is it possible to know how well a cricketer is bowling in a test match series? You would count the number of wickets he or she has bowled and compare that with the number of wickets a cricketer with a similar style, say a fast bowler, takes in a similar number of overs bowled.

In football, you'd count the number of goals a striker has scored and compare that to the number of goals other strikers in the same league have scored.

Again, I am oversimplifying it here to illustrate the point. Sporting achievement relies heavily on statistics and comparison. In the sports business, it's all about winning. The best, fairest way to determine the winner is to measure the performance.

Numbers don't lie, right? (Actually, numbers are often manipulated, but that's a topic for another time!)

So, where else is performance measured? Think about school. In the case of grades, students are awarded marks that teachers have determined are reflective of their work. The mark or the 'score' is benchmarked against the 'scores' of other students in which the average mark is determined, and a student's performance is assessed according to its relationship to the average.

These marks then help students understand how well (or not) they are performing in particular subjects. It provides them with an opportunity to ask for help, increase the level of disciplined study they incorporate into their routine or, in some cases, reject certain subjects that create a seemingly insurmountable struggle. Schools and other organisations like universities, colleges and internship programmes use these marks to determine students' suitability for particular programmes of interest.

If you think about it, it makes sense. It would be highly inappropriate to award someone entrance into medical school if they perform poorly at subjects like chemistry and biology, basic subjects that every good physician needs to grasp and apply. They have the lives of their patients in their hands, after all, and their ability to make a positive difference to someone's health depends upon them understanding basic bodily functions and physiological processes.

In business, a company measures its performance using a whole host of metrics, tracking everything from sales and profit margins to client satisfaction to talent attraction and retention. These metrics guide both business leaders and individual employees to adjust their strategies and tactics where necessary to augment the results they achieve.

Think about a salesperson. How would she measure her success? From a purely sales point of view, she would calculate the total value of sales over a period of time, say three months (known as a quarter in business).

While this is a good start, it is not always the best or most revealing measure. So, she might then determine how much profit (income minus expenses) she was able to achieve for the company with those sales.

Why is this important? If the salesperson spent a disproportionate amount of money acquiring her sales in relation to her colleagues, she and her company might want to look at the acquisition costs per customer.

It could suggest that she employed an efficient customer acquisition strategy if the profit figure is high. On the other hand, it may suggest an inefficiency if profit is low. In either case, it provides a valuable window into the efficacy of the salesperson's activities.

Your Relationship to Performance

I realise that this might be blindingly obvious to you, but I hope you see the point I'm making: measuring performance gives you the ability to assess your performance by examining and quantifying a set of results in an area of life.

You might be thinking, "So what? Who cares how well I am performing? Is it healthy to compare myself to other people anyway?"

Performance measures and comparisons are neither good nor bad in and of themselves. They are merely guides. What can make them occur as good or bad is entirely dependent upon your attitude towards the results and the particular area of life for which your performance is being measured.

It's this aspect of performance, your attitudinal position and relationship to the realm of performance itself, that is often omitted from performance discussions. It's your relationship to the reality of your performance, measured by the results you produce, that trips you up.

Let's face it. Confronting reality can be, well, confronting.

Have you ever tried to lose weight? Have you baulked at stepping on the scale every morning to track how much your body actually weighs?

I know I have. I used excuses like, "I judge my body by how I feel in clothes, not by how much I weigh," or "Muscle weighs more than fat, and I've been working out a lot, so of course I'll weigh a lot."

It's a great justification to avoid facing facts. When I get over it, stop making myself wrong for weight fluctuations (that's what the body *does*) and monitor it on a daily basis, I can take intentional action to manage my weight because I know what the reality *is*, not what I hope it is.

Consider that managing weight, like managing your quarterly sales figures or exam results, is a matter of performance. You get out what you put in. And you don't have to be naturally gifted at something to excel at it, despite what you might think.

Your attitude to performance determines the actions you take and the ability you develop to accomplish the things you want to accomplish in life. As an infant, you don't say to yourself, "I'll never be able to walk because I'm just not naturally good at it." No! You roll over, and then you push until you're on your knees, crawling. Or maybe you're a bum shuffler. The point is that you learn to move.

You develop the strength in your legs to hold yourself up. You start to pull yourself up. You learn balance. You take your first steps. You fall. You pick yourself up again and again until you are able to take several steps in a row. You discover the joys and freedom of walking.

And then you start to run! And you continue to fall and pick yourself up as you get stronger and more confident in your abilities to move. At this point, perhaps you add skills like dribbling a football or dancing ballet. And while you may still fall at times, you fall less and less.

The point I'm making is this: if you want to perform well at something, you've got to work at it. Rarely are people born good mathematicians or amazing runners. They continually take actions with the intention of stretching their performance results. In truth, the best performers compete with their previous performance rather than other people.

Tracking your performance by assessing results from a number of different angles helps you make the necessary adjustments, helping you to improve your performance. When you consider our discussion at the beginning of this chapter, especially the litany of questions I asked you to answer, I trust you are now starting to recognise the reason for it.

I can hear the pennies dropping as I write!

Reflect upon those questions again, but within the context of performance as an attitudinal position. Review your original answers and consider the following:

- What are you noticing as you reread what you've written?
- What themes become apparent?
- How would you describe your original attitude to performance?
- What, if anything, has changed since you originally answered the questions?
- How does that make you feel?
- Where and how is the feeling expressing itself in your mind, emotions and body?

You may already find this conversation difficult. Just the thought of having to track your performance makes you break out in a cold sweat.

I get it. I was just like you, and in some areas, I still am. Some people measure everything and take great pleasure in it. I know people who sheepishly admit they love spreadsheets and have them for everything.

Personally, I focus on one or two areas at a time until I have mastered the skill so that it occurs as natural. The measurement then becomes less confronting, more empowering and eventually unnecessary.

Why? Because I have the information, the *data*, that enables me to own the results.

Now, I advise you to create goals using the SMARTER method. Let's break down the acronym. SMARTER stands for Specific, Measurable, Achievable, Relevant, Time-based, Evaluated and Revised.

Why is this important? Having a goal like wanting to lose weight is nice, but it's conceptual. Creating a goal like losing 10 kilos by the end of March contains all the elements required for completion and feelings of accomplishment that accompany its fulfilment.

When you accomplish one goal, your intrinsic motivation increases, encouraging you to tackle new goals. It's a virtuous performance circle.

Reality Equals Opportunity

In this data-driven world, it can feel maddening to focus so much on numbers and results. It is only when you start to engage with data and learn how to extrapolate the information contained within it that it becomes exciting.

Equally, results in an external reality are not the only motivating factors. Too much emphasis on numbers, data and results can leave you feeling robotic. Soulless, even.

We human beings are far more complex than that. Sometimes we do things not because of the results produced but because of how it makes us *feel*. Sometimes we do things driven by a higher purpose, the results of which may not be realised in our lifetime. Think of all the people who have devoted themselves to curing cancer or getting humanity to Mars, for example.

The important thing, in my experience, is not to be driven by one at the exclusion of the other. Rather, I recommend you take a holistic approach to performance. To do that, you have to consider both intrinsic and extrinsic motivations.

In this book, we are going to focus primarily on your intrinsic motivation. There are a lot of great resources out there that can help you track the data to boost your extrinsic motivation already. What I intend to offer you is the opportunity to see how small shifts in thinking and feeling, or intrinsic motivating factors, can make a world of difference to your external performance.

Believe me. Being able to produce results in the external world - actually touching and feeling and seeing something you've produced - is a highly effective extrinsic motivator. It builds confidence, which feeds your intrinsic motivators, and you'll want to take on even bigger challenges.

Isn't that exciting?

I'd love to help you start with an area of life where you want to master performance and develop meaning that is appropriate for you. I'll guide you along the way, but the important thing is that you relate to your performance in a way that is meaningful to YOU.

This way of teaching and learning is called ontological teaching and learning. It's not what most people are used to. It certainly isn't the way we've all been taught in traditional learning environments. However, it is a way of learning through enquiry and discovery, which creates a more profound and lasting experience than being told what to think.

Why? It works because you own the teaching and learning in a way you wouldn't if I just spoon-fed you the information. You embody both teacher and student. You become your own coach.

The day you reach that stage is the day our work is done. It's a bittersweet moment, a little like getting a child settled into university. There's the thrill at his or her start to an independent life that's tinged with sadness at the thought of them being away from you.

But that's the job of the parent or guide. It's not to keep you trapped in a relationship but rather to equip you with the skills to navigate life on your own. You become your own boss, the master of your own life.

For the purposes of this book, you will be learning skills that enable you to be a master of your approach to performance in life. How difficult can it be? Just follow your heart, and you'll be happy.

Funny how it's never as straightforward as that. What do you think might be getting in the way? And what would it be like if you could simply remove the roadblocks to your progress with next-to-no effort?

Follow me to the next chapter, where I'll share a little of my transition into the world of self-mastery and healthy high performance.

Chapter 3

Mindfulness: What the Bleep Is it?

It was during my first spiritual retreat in the mid-1990s that I discovered the wonders of the vast field of human experience called mindfulness. A door to an entirely new world opened at that moment and I, being the adventurer I am, walked through it. I had no idea of the vast field of endeavour that awaited me.

I'm glad I did.

The mornings began with an outdoor class of qigong, a gentle Chinese martial art. The fact that people actually *chose* to exercise outside during a damp British summer was a revelation. Fairly soon after starting the class, I could understand why. The level of energy I felt in my body after performing several simple moves astonished me. It was as if I had been plugged into some mysterious energy source.

The experience of feeling, *really feeling* my feet on the dew-dampened grass, awakened my senses to a new world of human potential.

During one of the retreat's meditations, I explored the limits of consciousness by connecting deeply to the sense of hearing. I travelled to the ends of the universe and back with my mind in 30 minutes.

Mind. Blown.

I had no idea that my mind was capable of such amazing experiences. In exploring the mind's vastness all those years ago, I discovered the immense power we call mind that is innate in all human beings. I was captivated.

I also uncovered the deep mistruths that are continually fed to human beings about the nature of the mind and the power that it holds. Most people associate the intellect with the mind. However, the mind is far more complex and interesting than that. In fact, the mind is a bigger and more complicated organ than we realise. Understanding its complexities is a matter of personal discovery.

For people like me, plumbing its depths is a lifelong pursuit. My intention with this book is to share a little of what I've learned in a way that gets you started on the road to experiencing and truly knowing your own mind.

Mindfulness is a practice that enables human beings to go beyond the usual waking experience of the mind. The clue is in the name.

Mindfulness helps you access the *fullness* of the mind. It enables an experience that transcends the limitations of intellect and language. It's an expanded level of awareness that most are unaccustomed to experiencing, except on occasions when it is called into being by a special moment, like a breathtaking sunrise or the birth of a child.

When you experience it for the first time, you recognise it as extraordinary. The world slows down, colours amplify in their brightness, the body tingles with a variety of sensations and life takes on a patina of simplicity.

Why is it considered extraordinary?

Mindfulness ought to be a perfectly natural experience. The truth is, when you were conceived in your mother's womb, your spirit, mind, emotions and body operated as an integral whole.

And then… life happens.

Mindfulness… Interrupted

Remember when you were young without a care in the world? It's hard, isn't it? From the moment you start babbling, the adults around you expect things from you.

When is he going to turn over? Will she say, 'Mama' or 'Dada' first?

Learning life skills can prove challenging. Imagine how many times you had to fall over while learning to walk or struggle until you got the hang of going to sleep. This is expected of you.

And then, there are those instances when life doesn't quite go your way. When it doesn't, you react with emotional outbursts that a) overwhelmed you and b) provoked unexpected, undesirable results in yourself and those around you.

Ever had one of those thrashing, screaming temper tantrums? You may not remember it, but just about everyone on the planet has had the pleasure of vociferously making their desires known to anyone who will listen.

Imagine a person who is the picture of serenity. It could be someone you know, someone of legend or an imaginary person. Picture that person in your mind's eye. Notice how you feel when you think of this person.

Now, imagine this person as a child. See him or her as a toddler or a teenager having a tantrum. Maybe they're on the floor thrashing their limbs, sulking and slamming doors as they walk through the house or shouting at the top of their lungs about something trivial.

The point is this: very few people, even the people labelled legends, are born with wisdom. You acquire this quality as you move through life.

Wisdom develops by combining extrinsic motivation generated by an external circumstance with one's own internal 'stuff' about the circumstance, known as intrinsic motivation. Wisdom is not a finite thing. It grows and changes as you gain new knowledge and have new experiences.

More on wisdom later, but I trust you get the gist.

Experiencing difficult emotions like upset and frustration is typical of childhood, and it's perfectly understandable, given the fact that children's minds are developing and they are learning what the society they live in deems acceptable behaviour. Making mistakes and being guided to correct them is how human beings adapt to the cultural norms of their particular cultural society.

While this type of behaviour is acceptable in children, it's less than charming in adults. You may believe you should have it all sorted out by the time you reach 30.

Is that ever true of anyone? No. We are all a work in progress. Developing genuine wisdom takes continuous, conscious work at developing it. It doesn't just appear one day because you've reached a particular age. There is no limit to the level of wisdom you can acquire in life, either.

So, what happens when learning situations you encounter in childhood don't turn out for the best or the best as you see it? This can happen for a number of reasons, including lack of adequate guidance, accidents, challenging new people and expectations, and it happens to everyone.

Why is this relevant? You might think that your behaviour reflects that of an adult when in reality, you are making decisions from a childhood, and possibly childish, perspective.

Human beings have developed a whole variety of strategies over millennia to manage these experiences. Let's explore one of the most important of these strategies - dissociation.

Dissociation and the Formation of the Personality

One of the most prevalent and perhaps least understood strategies human beings have developed for managing painful or traumatic experiences is dissociation. The Oxford English Dictionary defines dissociation as 'the action of disconnecting or separating or the state of being disconnected.' [4]

It is, in fact, a very clever mechanism of consciousness that allows you to lift your conscious self out of a traumatic or painful situation to minimise the suffering.

Dissociation is a useful survival tool as long as the effort is made to reintegrate by acknowledging, accepting and transforming the impact of the experience. Problems arise when dissociation sticks as a way of being.

Children regularly experience situations that are overwhelming, and a way of dealing with the overwhelming thoughts, emotions and sensations is to dissociate or split off an aspect of their identity. Fear is at the source of them deciding they have to be a certain way to survive in life.

This is how what are known as personality traits are formed.

People believe dissociation comes with severe trauma and only occurs in people with mental disorders like dissociative identity disorder (DID), formally known as multiple personality disorder or MPD, or schizophrenia. This is not true. Almost all human beings have suffered an event that occurs as significant and dissociative, whether they see it as a positive or a negative experience.

In these moments, the human machinery called the body, with its emphasis on keeping you alive, concludes that your survival trumps wisdom. You, in turn, make decisions about how you have to behave to ensure your survival. Sometimes you define the circumstances under which you can have certain experiences. Personality traits develop as a result of these experiences. These experiences add a tint to the lens through which we view our lives.

These experiences are not simply limited to childhood, though. When the zygotes connected in your mother's womb, your life force kicked into action. That life force is the very substance that enlivens the whole universe.

Your parents provided you with the genetic blueprint that establishes a context in your life. Your job as a human being is to take what you've been provided and make the most of it.

Significant experiences can occur both in utero and once a child is born. Sometimes the phrase 'born this way' is kind of true. Foetuses respond to the environment in and around the womb, and they are intimately connected with their mothers. If the mother experiences trauma, it can impact the unborn child, just as the ingestion of toxic substances can affect the unborn baby's development. [5]

Each of these formative experiences, especially traumatic ones, creates a separation in the psyche, a fork in the road, carving out a route down which you travel again and again whenever you encounter a situation that provokes a similar reaction. Neuroscientists call these habitual patterns of thinking and their associated experiences neural pathways.

Imagine the firing of particular transmitters sets off a chain reaction of thoughts, images, memories, emotions, feelings, sensations, impulses and behaviours. That chain reaction repeats itself every time a familiar situation is encountered.

Of course, there is evidence to suggest that our genes carry the potential for us to have certain qualities, good and bad. However, environmental factors and your relationship to your environment determine whether or not the potential traits that lie dormant as an epigenetic marker activate and manifest as a full-blown personality trait.

Though some of the traits you've developed as a result of life experience serve you well, some definitely don't. And both are equally limiting. That sounds radical but think of it this way. Anything you regard as 'definite' is limiting because you consider it to be definitive.

Believing that a particular personality trait is an essential part of you and relying on it to succeed in life limits you even further. How? You have decided that the 'way you do it' is the best or only way for you to handle life. In reality, it is one of an infinite number of ways you can approach a situation.

Locking yourself into a particular way of being strips you of freedom, doesn't it? It imprisons you in a way of being that, if you're honest with yourself, doesn't give you any choice at all.

I hope you are starting to question your own personality, whatever it is you believe it to be. I invite you to wonder how aspects of your own personality formed. I trust you are starting to get curious about how to acquire some freedom to choose your way of being.

So, why do we do it? Why do we limit ourselves in this way?

The Correlation Between the Brain and Consciousness

It is a matter of the way your brain and consciousness collaborate.

Your brain helps you function in life with a minimal amount of conscious activity to create efficiency. Most of the actions you undertake are controlled by unconscious processes.

For example, you don't get up in the morning and say: 'Heart, it's time to beat at 80 bpm now that I'm awake and moving.' Your unconscious mind takes care of that for you. It is an inbuilt function of your physiology (the way in which a living organism or body part functions) to control the nervous system that sends the signal for your heart to increase its rate of beating as you rise and begin to move.

Similarly, you don't start from scratch every time you react. Your decisions are filed in your brain's memory bank, called the hippocampus. It especially likes to keep at the forefront of the filing cabinet those experiences that accompany a strong emotion like fear. When you next encounter a frightening situation, for example, the emotional centre of your brain - the limbic brain - refers to the fear files and their accompanying behavioural strategies. Those neural pathways associated with the chosen strategy start firing to deliver the behaviour that helped you survive last time.

This sounds perfectly reasonable, given that your brain is hardwired for survival, and it does a pretty good job at that. You've made it this far, haven't you?

So, what's the problem?

Surviving life and living life to its fullest potential exist in opposition to each other. Surviving life necessitates risk aversion, whereas performing to a high degree in life requires you to take risks. Surviving life requires you to fight, flee, freeze or fawn when you encounter a threat. High performance in life often calls on you to go beyond survival instincts to do something that exists 'outside the box' of the survival mentality.

In short, survival causes your life to contract, to get smaller. Thriving makes your life expand, giving you opportunities to discover yourself as a big person.

Do you want to accomplish things in life? Do you experience life fully, or do you feel pushed from pillar to post, from potential accomplishment to survival? Do you feel as though two halves of yourself are in a constant battle?

The latter question, describing an inner conflict, is a good example of a common case of dissociation. It reveals that we have different sides to our personality, each with differing motivations, needs and drives. As you move through life, you discover that this experience is prevalent in just about everyone.

While this may seem hopeless, it is possible to learn how to work with your machinery or your neurological system. You can achieve mastery in managing your emotions. You can learn how to overcome the survival strategies, take risks and achieve a level of life performance that right now may seem like a pipe dream.

The Chink in the Survival Armour

Now, while the armour of the survival instinct is strong, it is not impenetrable. In fact, it's easier to dismantle than you think.

So, how do you fulfil your goals in a way that leaves you with a sense of power, accomplishment and fulfilment?

How do you move from being a follower with minimal discernible power to showing up as an active participant making genuine contributions to the communities in which you operate?

Let me share with you how this worked in my own life. Before practising mindfulness, I was terrified of making mistakes, and this manifested in my first serious job. I was so scared that I avoided taking professional risks and instead spent a lot of time in bars with colleagues or journalists. Working in PR, I felt I had a fabulous excuse! The truth is, I was stuck in a rut, and I couldn't see a way out.

Two things got me out of the rut: insightful feedback from a director who said my perfectionism was crippling me; and regular mindfulness practice.

I went from being an account executive to an account director in a year, managing the company's internet services strategy. In that time, the company began to trust my judgement and acted on an early suggestion that they invest in internet technology companies. This led the agency to triple in size in three years.

Mindfulness made a significant contribution to my ability to turn things around. I started going to bed early. I got to work early. I took responsibility for my perfectionist thought patterns, and I shared my ideas freely. In doing so, I created success in my career for the first time.

Here's how it worked for a client of mine who had been out of work for two years after the death of a loved one. She and I used mindfulness techniques to help her see what was really at the source of her depression - self-pity. She saw that her attitude of feeling sorry for herself created the spiral down the bottomless emotional pit of powerlessness and hopelessness.

In discovering this, she chose to embrace new ways of thinking. This radically altered her mood and her experience of life. Within five weeks of starting our coaching sessions together, she landed the perfect job. In her words, our sessions helped her "get her sparkle back."

If applying mindfulness can do that for me and it can do it for my clients, it can absolutely do it for you.

Have I sold you on the virtues of mindfulness yet? Whether you are a 'yes' or 'no', I invite you to keep reading and keep writing to build the foundation for approaching high performance in a mindful way.

Chapter 4

Sheep, Donkey, Bee or Human?

Let's explore this by looking at how performance tends to function within the context of business. While I am using the example of business here, you can apply what I'm saying to other contexts - schools, religion, political movements, social media and so on. Understanding this will help you consciously choose how to interact with your environment. This will enable you to improve your performance in ways you haven't yet considered. It's all part of the journey to self-mastery in life.

Business has traditionally designed processes with the intention of driving behaviours that contribute to creating efficiencies and success for the company. This seems to be the mantra by which most human resources (HR) or people departments live.

What do you hear in that statement? Here's what comes to my mind: a field full of sheep being herded by a few nippy sheep dogs that corral their woolly 'friends' inside a designated fence. Once inside the fence, Big Daddy sheepdog, the farmer, locks the gate and keeps the sheep there until the next go at rounding them up and herding them in a particular direction. The sheepdog gets rewarded with a treat from Big Daddy, while the sheep just get sheared.

It's not an image of empowerment really, is it? And yet, when I attend HR conferences and I hear people sharing their 'success' stories, this is what my mind conjures up. There's very little concern for individual fulfilment and more concern for rolling out more sophisticated carrot-and-stick systems designed to 'drive behaviours.'

Are you one of those sheep? Maybe you're a beast of burden, like a donkey? Personally, I know I am definitely a human being, and if you're reading this, you are human, too. Clearly, you're neither sheep nor donkey, but do you behave like one? Does your company expect you to behave like one?

Risking stating the blindingly obvious, human beings, while sharing biological traits with our animal friends, are distinctly different from sheep and donkeys and all other creatures in significant ways.

We have been gifted with an upright body that gives us greater mobility and an enhanced brain that enables us to solve super complex problems and create amazing things. We've been given the gifts of reason and imagination. We can rise above survival instincts and make conscious choices about how to participate in life with intention. We share a large proportion of our DNA with most creatures on the planet, but we can make very different use of our minds and our physiology.

Isn't it a little curious, then, that behavioural psychologists propose theories designed to appeal to the animalistic side of human nature?

For example, the 'hive mind,' a buzzword often seen as attractive by large organisations, appeals to the basest level of human consciousness.

Did you know you're not an insect, either? You might buzz around the office at times, or perhaps you wear fairy wings at a work's fancy-dress party, but you're not an insect. Again, I'm stating the obvious, but I feel it needs to be said.

You are a brilliant human being. Acknowledge yourself for it!

Obviously, businesses must work, and systems certainly help to create an environment of workability. However, appealing to the animalistic side of humanity does not create satisfaction and career fulfilment, the ideal environment for high performance to naturally occur. Instead, it dehumanises people, leaving them with the experience of being drones, beasts of burden, or a source of food and clothing.

What's the solution?

Know Thyself and the Environment Around You

The first step is to recognise what's occurring, and what's occurring is often a lack of understanding of a system's purpose. Purpose is a higher-minded cognitive function that appeals to the human part of your brain. When you understand the purpose of something and how it fits into the overall picture of the business, you're much more likely to willingly participate in the system.

Think back to our earlier discussion about performance measurements. You may recognise resistance to measuring performance. For example, you may actively avoid looking at exam results, a project plan or your bank balance. Instead of sticking your head in the sand, I invite you to get curious about the conversations inside your head that create the resistance.

Let's take your own experience of the business or environment you're currently in. Are there activities you object to doing? In consultancy businesses, for example, timesheets can be a regular source of irritation.

If this is a source of complaint for you, ask yourself:

- What's your biggest complaint about timesheets?
- What emotion arises when you think about timesheets?
- What physical sensation arises as you think about timesheets?
- What urges or impulses arise as you think about timesheets?
- How does this complaint influence your behaviour around timesheets?
- What impact does this behaviour have on you, your team, your department and your company?
- Finally, what is the purpose of timesheets?

If timesheets are not a source of complaint for you, replace them with something that is. The purpose of this questioning is not to examine timesheets. The purpose is to examine *your relationship* to timesheets or any other regular task that irritates you.

If you are working on an area of performance not related to business - academic performance, for example - replace timesheets with a task that frustrates you like revision, writing essays or sitting exams.

We're going to return to the matter of practices like timesheets, revision and measurements later in the book. I want to illustrate the fact that you have a relationship with everything, both animate and inanimate. If you are unaware of the dynamics of your relationship with something, you have no power in that relationship.

Ever heard the phrase, knowledge is power? My own version of that phrase is mindfulness is power. It gives you greater choice by providing access to both inner and outer information. Inner knowledge, in particular, is generally not available to you when you operate on autopilot.

Of particular value to you is knowing yourself. It comes about by bringing to light the aspects of yourself that were hidden from your view, developing a relationship with that part of yourself, and working with it to achieve excellence.

Let's take this discussion a little further. Ask yourself the following questions and record your answers in your journal. In answering these questions, I advise you to be both straight and free with yourself.

What inspires me to create success:

- For myself personally?
- For others?
- As part of a community?
- As part of my company or industry?

- As part of my country?
- For the human race?

I don't expect you to have it all figured out yet and there are no right or wrong answers. The idea is to speculate about what matters to you as you expand into each of the realms.

What do you notice?

I'm asking you to take yourself through a special kind of process, a process that encourages you to be mindful of how you relate to yourself and the impact this relationship has on the way you relate to others and the world around you. What occurs on the outside reflects what's occurring on the inside.

The Limitations in Giving Advice

A lot of personal development in the market today provides you with strategies to deal with certain situations. 'Follow this format to get that promotion.' 'Use this tool to marry the partner of your dreams.'

Sound familiar?

In what realm does all of this advice exist?

It exists within the realm of behavioural change. It's an approach that deals with behaviour and external results, and it comes from the head of another person, not yours. There is nothing wrong with it. It's just that there's more focus on action than consideration. More importantly, there's little of the ownership that comes naturally when you exercise creativity to solve problems for yourself.

Action alone will not create the results you desire. It's important that you grasp the context in which you're operating, the impact you intend to have and the results you set out to realise. It's one of the reasons I ask you constant questions. I want you to discover YOUR intrinsic and extrinsic motivations. It's much more powerful when it comes from you.

Now, it's tempting to start with the big picture and work your way down. While it is important to have a sense of vision, you also need to have a clear, truthful view of your starting point, in our case, the reality of your performance at a moment in time.

Consider the following:

- What beneficial skills and gifts do you have in your personal toolbox?
- How might these skills and gifts shape the way in which you create success?
- What gaps in your skillset would you like to fill?
- How do you assess the impact your actions have on your accomplishments?
- What will you alter to create desired results?

You can answer all these questions powerfully and still not create the results you desire. The reason is simple. There will be areas of dissociation in your 'personality' that block you from taking action in a powerful, intentional way. Until you uncover these hidden barriers and create alternatives that support your goals, you'll feel frustrated and thwarted, as if you're moving through treacle.

Now do you understand why that personality conversation was so important? This is how ontological learning works. I present you with something, giving you the opportunity to grapple with it before I reveal the answer.

If you were mindful of your thoughts, you might have already understood how the personality conversation influences our discussion. Having it confirmed gives you a boost of self-confidence and trust in your own wisdom.

If you didn't get there yourself, do not fear. That's why you're here, reading this book.

What ingredient helps you build self-confidence and self-mastery?

Mindfulness Completes the Picture

Mindfulness is the first step in mastering the mental processes that fuel your behaviour. Behaviouralists may want you to believe that the bulk of your behaviour is determined by external or extrinsic motivating factors.

It can be. While focusing on the external is a good way to determine results that show up in reality, focusing solely on extrinsic motivation creates a one-sided, dissociated view of the whole realm of behaviour itself.

Behaviour, at its root, is determined by your thoughts, conscious and unconscious, about your relationship to yourself and both your internal experience and external environment. These thoughts trigger emotional reactions. The emotional reactions fuel impulses, which influence behaviour. Behaviour drives action. Action produces results. To transform your results, you must transform your thoughts: the source of all your behaviours.

Mindfulness enables you to master your own behaviour by mastering the source of your behaviour - your thoughts - and aligning your thoughts with your results. Mindfulness mastery comes with practice, and once learned, you will be equipped to apply these skills to master your behaviour and determine your own behaviours at a moment's notice.

Mindfulness helps you respond to situations by taking in and assessing information from a number of sources before taking action. When you become adept at mindfulness, you will be able to accomplish this in seconds.

The value in learning mindfulness is that, in mastering your own behaviours by learning to *respond* rather than *react*, you learn to create desirable outcomes that serve you and those around you.

By building mindfulness techniques into your daily routine, you begin to incorporate mindfulness as a way of being until it feels as natural and habitual as brushing your teeth.

Why? Because it works.

Let me share an example of this with you. One of my clients, a successful businesswoman, was struggling with her job as a consultant. She raced from one job to another, rarely finding time for her family and friends. She didn't need to work, but she couldn't seem to break the habit of putting work above all else. The constant chasing of the next big thing was proving increasingly frustrating and ultimately unfulfilling.

I asked her what it would be like for her to incorporate moments in her day where she "stopped to smell the roses."

She gasped and exclaimed, "I never do that." I invited her to try it on for a few weeks.

When she returned for the next session, she looked decidedly different. She realised that her job was not working for her, so she resigned. It was as if a two-ton weight had been lifted from her shoulders.

What's interesting about this situation? Well, for me, she was failing to do what a lot of people fail to do in business. She forgot to breathe in. She was so focused on delivering results in the outer world that she failed to check in with herself to ensure her outer experience aligned with her inner desires.

In her case, it didn't. The gap between her inner and outer worlds was so uncomfortable she felt compelled to take action. This gave her access to determine what she really wanted from her life. In doing so, she found a job that met all of her requirements and worked around her life.

Let's go back to the whole idea of breathing. Remember that breathing is a two-way process. You breathe in, and you breathe out. If you do one without the other, you die. It's really simple.

Life is like that, too. You take action and deliver results, and then you evaluate those results against your desires and dreams.

Except that this is the ideal. Most people just take action. They don't take the time to evaluate whether or not the actions they are taking are producing the results they desire.

They are taking one long breath out and forgetting to breathe in again. This is why your experience of life can feel like it's draining your life force and deadening your spirit.

High performers share the ability to galvanise the energy needed to accomplish things. While this is something to be celebrated, it can be detrimental. High performers have the tendency to force results, sometimes at a high cost, like burnout or injury.

At this point, I want you to consider that results are not just measured in numbers. Results can also be measured by how you feel about a given circumstance or situation. You can be great at something and be miserable doing it. To be whole and complete, it is important that you give equal importance to your internal AND external reality. You must breathe in to breathe out.

How do you bring balance to this? When you remove forcefulness, you *allow* things to emerge. Have you heard the story of the person who thought he was helping free a butterfly from its cocoon? He prematurely pried open the cocoon. The butterfly died.

Some things need to be given the space to show up in their own time and way. They cannot be forced and remain alive and well, like the butterfly.

I want to help you bring aliveness to your life. Breath is life. It is the secret to all life. When you discover it, you will be amazed by its power. However, you can't discover this through intellect. Your learning will come from the direct experience of the power of consistent application of mindfulness. Experience is your greatest teacher.

I realise I have talked a lot about experience. I hope I have done a good job of setting the scene for what's to come for you. It's important to me that I leave you with an embodied experience of mindfulness and its high performance potential.

Stop for a moment, grab your journal, take three deep breaths in and out and then let your breathing come to its natural rhythm. Now ask yourself, "What have I discovered so far about my own relationship to performance?"

Record what arises for you. Things you could consider include:

- How has my perspective on performance changed?
- What new actions are opening up?
- What new possibilities are arising?
- How do I feel about incorporating mindfulness as a daily habit?
- What expectations do I have with regard to mindfulness's impact on my performance?

Taking the time to answer these questions will prepare the groundwork for experiencing the benefits of mindfulness in the next chapter.

Are you ready? Let's continue.

Chapter 5

Bringing Mindfulness Into Being

Mindfulness, like anything else you do regularly, works best when it becomes an integral part of how you operate. To convert beneficial behaviours into habits that stick requires consistent, committed practice at generating the thoughts that power the behaviour.

For busy people, the temptation is often to try to make it all happen in one sitting.

But consider this.

Imagine telling your dentist that you can't understand why your mouth is full of cavities when you brush your teeth seven times in the morning and seven times in the evening every Saturday. You wouldn't dream of it, would you?

Mindfulness operates in exactly the same way. For the practice of mindfulness to become an embedded habit, a way of being, you must make a commitment to practise it regularly.

Being realistic, I know that there are times when you go to bed without brushing your teeth. And I know there will be times when you can't find the space to integrate mindfulness practices into your day.

What I want you to do, in these instances, is to bring mindfulness to the equation. Ask yourself, 'What is *really* getting in the way of me taking a moment to breathe and just notice? What is *really* stopping me from taking the next step?'

Make a note, either mental or written, of what you discover. Then, get back on the horse and set off again. It really is that simple.

Remember that mindfulness is about connection.

Connecting with yourself mindfully will radically alter your connections with the world around you.

I recommend that you relate to each of the following chapters as a coaching session. What do I mean by that? Well, take one chapter, follow the instructions and apply what you've learned for a week or two. Once you feel accomplished with that chapter's exercise, start on the next one. Each exercise builds on the previous one. Dedicated application of the exercises will have you being mindful as a matter of habit in no time.

We are about to learn some mindfulness techniques that will help you start the process of self-mastery. You'll discover the power of your breath through some simple exercises.

Before we start breathing, let's examine the idea of working with life force.

Accessing Universal Life Force

In the previous chapter, we discussed the merits of connecting with both cycles of your breath - breathing in and breathing out.

The cycles of breath mirror the cycles of life. Think of the ocean waves. The tide comes in and it goes out, and it repeats this action over and over again.

For you to increase your performance in a profound way, you must be in touch with the entirety of you. That includes your inner world as well as the outer world. Most people only focus on increasing performance in the outer world, and while they may generate an improvement in results, their performance increases are incomplete.

Understanding, appreciating and working with the rhythms of breath gives you access to a whole new realm of performance, which you'll discover as your mindfulness experience unfolds.

The essence of all mindfulness practices lies in your connection with your breath. Why?

Breathing is a bodily function that generally happens unconsciously. The beauty of the breath is that when you consciously engage with the process of breathing, you notice the effects breathing has on your state of mind and overall well-being.

The breath carries the vital components of health; the in breath brings oxygen to power your cells, and the out breath expels carbon dioxide and other waste products.

Connecting to your breath allows you to observe the flow of life - taking in, absorbing, integrating and releasing. It is a flow you find in nature. Think of seasonal changes. Or consider your relationship with plant life. Remember that your exhalation of carbon dioxide feeds the plants, which in turn exhale oxygen, the life-giving element that promotes health for humans and animals.

The natural flow of life is not linear; it is torus-shaped, like a ring doughnut. You reach out to your environment, exchanging information and substances, you take these things in, you integrate them into your experience, you release what's not needed and you reach out to interact with your environment again. This constant exchange of information flows in and out, the movement creating an energy field. Your respiratory system acts as bellows that power the flow and stoke the internal fires of energy to keep things moving.

Once you begin to observe life as it naturally occurs, you are able to relate to it naturally. You acknowledge the interdependence of everyone and everything. You take an interest in the well-being of your environment, knowing that your own well-being depends upon it.

The Breath as the Connective Force

By connecting to the breath, you discover the interdependence between the various functions of your own being. Bringing consciousness to the breath enables you to connect your mind with your body and emotions.

The breath acts as the connective force. It provides the link that ties everything together, and it's an aspect of your physiology over which you have some conscious control.

When relating to your breath, it is useful to begin by merely observing it. Don't force it. Don't change it. Merely observe yourself in the act of breathing. Gentle mindfulness will take you much further than forceful mindfulness.

The act of observing your breath hones your observational skills, which you will need to develop to connect powerfully and consciously with your body. It works best to build your relationship with your breath and yourself gradually over time, so we will start slowly and build on each exercise.

In the beginning, bringing awareness to your breath can create a dramatic change in your state of being. You may notice feelings of slowing down, heaviness, dizziness or other phenomena. I advise you to do these exercises sitting down. If you feel light-headed, move your hands and feet in circles or give your body a quick shake to help you shift your awareness.

This is perfectly natural, by the way. Our natural way of being is light, like the breath. Mindfulness helps you reconnect to the lighter part of you. This will all become clearer as you move through the exercises in this book.

Would you like to experience mindfulness for yourself? If so, find a quiet space and try the following exercise.

Exercise One – Connecting With the Breath

Step One: Set a timer for two minutes.

Step Two: Close your eyes and focus on your breath. Don't try to change it. Just notice what happens as you bring your attention to your breath for two minutes.

Step Three: When the timer stops, open your eyes and notice what you're experiencing.

- What did you notice?
- What effect did the attentive breathing have on your thoughts?
- Your emotional state?
- Your physical state?
- Your experience of life itself?

Some of you may notice a heaviness that you're unaccustomed to, while others may feel a lightness. Some of you may experience a slowing down, while others may notice a speeding up. Some of you might feel calm, while others may feel anxious.

There are no right or wrong ways to experience mindfulness. Your way will be your way. The important thing is that you become acquainted with who YOU are.

Make sense?

What's Occurring?

You may be asking yourself the question: 'What is happening here? What is it that I'm doing by focusing so much attention on my breath?'

Ask yourself, 'What impact has observing my breath had on me?'

A way to appreciate the breath is to realise that breathing keeps you in constant contact with the flow between the external and the internal. The way you breathe mirrors the way you interact with the world and with yourself.

Consider the following:

- How conscious of yourself are you?
- How conscious of your body are you?
- How conscious of your mind and body relationship are you?
- How conscious of your emotional reactions are you?
- How conscious are you as you relate to external reality?
- How conscious are you of the effects external reality has on your internal reality?
- How conscious are you of the effects your internal reality has on external reality?

In short, how conscious are you of you?

Though that seems like a lot of questions, certain aspects of you are communicating with you all the time. How often do you listen?

Your body, your emotions and your thoughts are amazing sources of wisdom. Using all three aspects of your experience as a human being is a powerful route to accessing your unconscious mind. Using mindfulness to bring the unconscious to consciousness helps you reclaim your power from the buried neural networks of thought patterns and associated emotions, feelings, sensations and behaviours.

The breath is the primary mechanism that enables your mind to consciously connect with your body and emotions. When you create a strong link between mind, emotions and body, you develop and strengthen important functions that support high performance activities, like decision-making.

Connecting with the breath lets you operate with integrity, with a wholeness and completeness that you don't have when you operate solely from the mind. Let me illustrate what I mean by that.

You have heard the phrase: 'I trust my gut.' Did you know that your intestine contains neurons that are similar to those in the brain?

Now, you may trust your gut, but do you consult your heart? Often, we hear of a conflict between the head and the heart. Well, our hearts also contain neurons similar to those in our brains.

Your brain is your central source of information processing, but it doesn't work alone. It sends and receives signals from across the body, gathering feedback from your whole physiology. When you relate to every part of your body as an important information provider, you understand just how valuable a tool it is.

The purpose of mindfulness practices is to train you to powerfully create a link with your whole self. Bringing your attention down and into the body brings remarkable results on many levels.

Again, I could tell you what to expect, but that would be defeating the object of this book. Instead, I invite you to be open to what you discover.

I advise that you do all three exercises in this chapter. Each exercise builds upon the previous one. Ultimately, you'll discover which exercises work best for you. How can you determine which ones those are? By trying them out, of course! Remember, experience is your greatest teacher.

Exercise Two – Connecting the Breath With the Chest

Step One: Set a timer for two minutes

Step Two: Close your eyes and follow your breath's natural rhythm. Don't try to change it. Just follow it for a few breaths.

Step Three: Begin to notice your breath filling up your entire chest cavity as you breathe in. Notice how your chest moves as you breathe in and out of the chest cavity.

Step Four: Feel your breath filling up the chest first from bottom to top. Next, notice the breath filling up your chest both front to back, and finally, notice your breath filling up your chest side to side.

Step Five: Breathe out completely through the mouth. Repeat this breath cycle until the time is up.

Step Six: Open your eyes, sit quietly for a moment, and notice what you are experiencing in the moment.

What did you notice? What effect did breathing fully into your chest have on your thoughts? Your emotions? Your bodily sensations? Your physical state? Your view of life itself?

Let's take your breath a little deeper.

Exercise Three – Connecting the Breath With the Belly

Step One: Set a timer for three minutes

Step Two: Close your eyes and follow your breath's natural rhythm. Don't try to change it. Just follow it.

Step Three: Feel your breath filling up your entire chest cavity as you breathe in. Notice how your chest moves as you breathe in and out of the chest cavity, filling up the chest from bottom to top, front to back and side to side.

Step Four: Breathe out completely through the mouth. Repeat this breath cycle for about a minute.

Step Five: As you breathe in, notice the breath entering your belly cavity (the area between your ribcage and hips). Allow your belly cavity to fill up completely with your breath. You will feel the expansion of your belly in all directions as you breathe in and the contraction of your belly as you breathe out. Do this for a few breaths.

Step Six: When your belly cavity fills up, fill up your chest with air, taking it all the way to the top of your torso. When you exhale, empty your belly and chest gently and completely. Do this until the timer goes.

Step Seven: Open your eyes, sit quietly, and notice what you are experiencing in the moment.

What did you notice? What was the experience of going deeper each time? What effect did bringing your breath all the way down into your abdomen have on your thoughts? Your emotions? Your physical state? Your view of life itself?

Again, your experience is fine, right and proper for you whatever it is. There is no one way to experience the effects of deep breathing.

The Benefits of Breathing Deeply and Mindfully

Why is deep breathing important? As well as oxygenating the body, deep breathing activates the parasympathetic nervous system, the nervous system that sits in the driver's seat of bodily functions when the body is in a state of rest. Its opposite, the sympathetic nervous system, grabs the wheel in times of perceived danger and stress.

Some situations need the sympathetic nervous system to be activated, for instance when you need to be alert. At times, it's good to feel a little nervous, especially in situations in which high performance is required, like delivering a sales presentation, sitting a driving test or going on a first date.

It is an issue of the degree of alertness you feel. If you feel overwhelmed or hypervigilant, deep belly breathing will help you minimise the effects of the adrenaline and cortisol, your stress hormones that get released with the activation of the sympathetic nervous system.

Once the perceived threat or the stressful situation has passed, it is a good idea to breathe deeply for a moment or two to switch to a state of relaxation. Consciously acknowledging that you have 'survived' the situation and letting go of the anxiety helps bring you back to a state of peace and relaxation.

Remember to keep your breathing slow and gentle. This is not a race to get as much oxygen inside your body as possible. Believe it or not, too much oxygen creates more problems than it solves. That's why it's important to limit the time and keep it soft and natural.

As a high performer, you will almost certainly have times when you 'smashed it,' whatever the 'it' is. In these moments, take a few deep belly breaths in and out, filling your whole body with the experience of accomplishment and celebrate in whatever form it takes for you.

This one small act of kindness towards yourself can make a world of difference to future performance.

Finally, remember to record your experiences in your journal. Taking the time to do this will help you embed the experience.

Let's take it to the next level by learning to connect your breath and body with your behaviour.

Chapter 6

Connecting Breath, Body and Behaviour

Mindfulness, like any new habit, takes practice, commitment and *reminders* to make it a regular part of your day. After many years, I naturally incorporate it into my daily routine. However, it was not like that in the beginning.

If you're struggling to practise mindfulness regularly, I invite you to be mindful of your internal conversations around it. Judging yourself is unproductive. Forcing yourself to do it is unproductive. Avoiding the conversation with yourself is unproductive.

Being straight with yourself is productive. Taking action to honour your commitment to yourself is productive. Forgiving yourself when you lack commitment is productive.

You always have choice. Which way do you choose to go?

Stop for a moment to reflect on what you've done so far. How is your mindfulness practice going?

What impact are these exercises having upon you? Are you finding it difficult to commit to performing the exercises every day? If so, what is getting in the way? If you found that you were fully committed, what's that like?

It's valuable to assess the benefits and results of doing something once you've done it, like returning from a mining expedition and examining the gems you extracted. In our case, your 'gems' are the treasures that your mind and body hold.

Practise, Practise, Practise

Practice helps you incorporate mindfulness into your day. Practice prepares you to reach the stage at which you can remain in a state of mindfulness most of the time. The intention is that you discover the benefits of mindfulness for yourself and choose how to make it part of your waking experience.

Like any habit or skill, it takes time to develop, it takes regular practice to get good at it, and it takes experimentation for you to find your own way of accessing mindfulness.

What does mindfulness provide you? I'm sure you've already reaped a number of benefits, like enhanced relaxation, focus and observational skills. Have you noticed a difference in your performance in a particular area of life?

Here's a little secret. The more you can acknowledge yourself for even the tiniest of accomplishments, the more you'll improve your performance. Even if you've only practised the previous exercises once, I want you to stop and acknowledge yourself for having made a start.

Go on. Have a go. Just notice what it's like to give yourself a metaphorical pat on the back.

Why am I asking you to do this?

One of the more exciting benefits of mindfulness lies in the doorway it opens to the whole, largely undiscovered world of you as a human being. Through the practices of mindfulness, you regard yourself more completely than you would without it. You take into consideration a new realm of information that, without mindfulness, wouldn't be available to you.

You recognise how brilliant you already are and have the potential to be, which your mind, body and environment are communicating to you. It gives you an opportunity to stop and be thankful for these little nuggets of self-recognition and self-worth.

Responding or Reacting

What's the value of bringing mindfulness to subtle aspects of communication?

Mindfulness awakens your senses, including the sixth sense, often called intuition. What does intuition mean to you? Some call it gut instinct. For me, it's a knowing that can't be explained through senses or fact.

It's an internal wisdom that most of us have. However, when you are too focused on the external world, you don't hear or regard the voice of intuition, an important tool in your sensory toolkit.

Intuition, in turn, enables you to make informed decisions based on an expanded set of information. This helps you to respond to situations rather than react to them, increasing your ability to respond to yourself and the world around you with a considerable degree of power.

Why is that important? Let's look at how this works by comparing the words 'react' and 'respond', which I alluded to in an earlier chapter. It's time to assess the virtues of reacting and responding.

'React' is exactly what it suggests: something that you act out over and over again. It's an automatic response to something. The word stems from the Latin *reagere*, which literally means 'to do or perform again'. [6]

How often do you find yourself reacting to things in the same way? Perhaps your boss criticises your work and you shy away from taking risks. Or a friend invites you at 5pm on Friday to a party that night and you get annoyed because you really want to go but you've already got plans.

Don't beat yourself up about it. Everyone has these moments. How well are they working for you, though?

You might think, 'This is just who I am. This is my personality.'

Remember what I said about the development of your personality? I'd argue that your survival mechanism and a fear-based programme have automatically kicked in and are driving your personality.

In the case of the critical boss, what fear could be at the source of shying away from risk? In the case of a last-minute invitation, what fear could be at the source of the annoyance at being unable to participate in a social situation?

When you acknowledge the fear that lies under the thought patterns and resulting behaviours, notice what comes up. Ask yourself, "Is my survival really at risk, or is something else going on? When did this fear begin?"

'Respond', on the other hand, originates from the Latin *respondere*, meaning to 'pledge again'. [7]

The Cambridge English Dictionary defines a pledge as 'a formal promise or something that is given as a sign that you will keep a promise'. [8]

The difference is significant here. Can you see it? To respond requires you to operate from a different level of consciousness. To pledge or promise something again, you need to be aware of what you've already promised. Being mindful of your promises gives you choice to make the promise a second time or to change your promise to better suit the situation.

Reacting, on the other hand, suggests action without thought. There's no promise or commitment to it. It's simply behaving the way you've always behaved. You allow the existing neural pathways to determine your course of action.

Reacting does not offer a lot of choice or power, does it? You can justify your behaviour and absolve yourself of responsibility, but it's not going to produce elevated performance.

What Are Your Promises?

Consider that if you want to create different results, you will need to make new promises that fuel a different set of actions. Which way of being will help you take a different set of actions to create a different set of results - reacting or responding?

You'd choose to respond every single time, wouldn't you?

Consider the kind of performance results responding would help you create that you haven't already created. How would this make you feel?

Now, often you will find yourself in a position in which you have to respond without all the information you need. This is especially true when it comes to making decisions. It creates uncertainty which can leave you doubting your ability to be effective.

This is the source of a lot of self-doubt. You probably assume that external factors make you doubt yourself but notice what you have learned about internal factors like promises and the impact they can have on your ability to make decisions. It's hard to truly respond when you're not conscious of the promises you've already made to yourself and others.

Think about the impact on your relationships, for example, when you break your promises by reacting rather than responding. Imagine cancelling on a pre-arranged dinner date with one set of friends, using a fabricated excuse because a 'better' offer crops up at the last minute.

If you're willing to be authentic with yourself, you'll admit that succumbing to FOMO (fear of missing out) doesn't leave you or others feeling good about your actions. In fact, it erodes trust.

Here's the good news. You can always come clean and recreate your promise in the process, providing you know what the original promise was. When you respond according to your promises and truthfully communicate these promises, you build trust in yourself being a person of your word. Your promises increase in efficacy when they are grounded in action.

That's powerful. That enables you to trust you. It enables others to trust you.

Responding Versus Reacting in Action

Let me illustrate what I mean. While I'm using a business scenario here, it is applicable to all sorts of interactions with others, so feel free to substitute the scenario with one familiar to you.

Imagine you are in a meeting, and your client asks you to do something. Your head says, 'Agree. She's the client, and what the client says, goes.' Your heart says, 'I don't agree but I don't want to upset her.' Your stomach says, 'There is something wrong with this request.'

What's your first inclination? Would you listen to head, heart or gut? And what's your promise in this instance?

Sometimes, your first impulse may be the right one. Sometimes, it's not the right one. What are you risking by always reacting rather than responding?

Consider that your client has come to you for your expertise. She is expecting you to advise her on the best way forward.

Your head says that your opinion will be unwelcome and threaten her authority. But your gut is warning you that things could go wrong if you don't share your concerns. Your heart wants to give her the honest answer because it feels like the right thing to do but without upsetting her.

Who stands to suffer if you ignore one message for the sake of the others? Potentially, you all suffer, especially if you ignore the red flags that your heart and gut are waving at you.

So, what could your heart and gut be telling you? Perhaps you need to probe a little more before you agree to something. Sometimes clients don't always fully comprehend the information you need to have to hand to fulfil your side of the arrangement - the promise. Maybe you have some industry knowledge that could contradict what your client is telling you, and you want to be able to share this without undermining your client's authority.

It could be anything, and it could be the very thing that your client wants and needs from you.

If you fail to listen to all the information being presented to you - in this case internal information coming from your head, heart and gut - you may not be providing your client with the expertise she is expecting from you. You are not honouring the fullness of your wisdom or your promise in this situation.

What's a likely outcome?

The messages from your head, heart and gut could be meaningless, and they could mean the difference between a failure, a little success and a lot of success. If you ignore them, you'll never know.

However, if you choose to operate from a state of mindfulness, taking a moment to reflect, listen and act on all the information you're given, how might you handle the situation?

For a start, you'd have to listen to the messages your head, heart and gut are telling you. In doing so, you will probably discover that your promise to serve the client's best interests is far more important than serving your own concerns about undermining her authority.

In accepting that your client wants your honest feedback and that she has come to YOU as an expert in your particular field, you might investigate the request further to get a fuller picture of what is being asked of you. You could tell your client straight that something feels a little out of kilter, sharing what you know and asking for clarity so that you can fully commit to delivering what's being asked of you.

You might have to reject the request if it is truly inappropriate. Handled as a reaction, this might upset your client but handled as a response, you will probably gain your client's respect for being forthright with your industry insight.

Which would you choose?

This kind of powerful relationship is possible when you take into account everything being communicated to you and learn to trust yourself in the process. When you learn to trust yourself, others learn to trust you, too.

This is a fairly basic example, but it happens in life all the time. In fact, many people are so unaware of what their bodies are saying to them that the head, heart and gut messages don't even register.

Consider this all in the context of performance. Remember, good performance is about the ability to deliver results. In business, your company or client hires you expecting a certain level of performance from you. What would it be like if you could not only meet expectations but exceed them and do it all with greater ease?

Brilliant performance is about offering and *being* a contribution in these exchanges. Responses enable more complete and valuable contributions.

Who do you choose to be, a responder or a reactor? Let's explore it in an exercise.

Practising Mindfulness Is Like Brushing Your Teeth

With mindfulness, you can explore how to deal with situations like this *in the moment*. You start by strengthening the link between mind and body. That's exactly what you'll be doing by bringing mindfulness to a basic task like brushing your teeth!

Bringing your full attention to your breath and your body as you perform basic tasks like brushing your teeth opens your awareness simply and easily. The misconception is that you achieve mindfulness through meditation only.

Mindfulness is a way of being that can be applied to every single activity you undertake, even sleeping. That is an advanced state of mindfulness, so let's start by bringing mindfulness to a task that I trust you perform at least twice a day, and that is brushing your teeth. If not, now is the perfect time to start.

As you prepare to brush your teeth, you will learn a quick technique for grounding to enable you to be fully aware of yourself in a standing position. This is an exercise that masters like martial artists learn at the beginning of their training to spread their awareness throughout their bodies. It is grounding that gives them the exquisite sensitivity needed to pre-empt and meet strikes from their opponents with mastery.

I can't promise you'll be a ninja by the end of the book. I can assure you, though, that learning the art of grounding helps you become aware of information in your environment that is not available when you concentrate your attention in your head.

We're doing this with an exercise like brushing your teeth, as I'm hoping it's a task you perform at least twice a day. By all means, don't feel you have to limit yourself to teeth brushing, though. I recommend you bring mindfulness to all habitual tasks like washing dishes or taking out the trash. There's a whole world of discovery waiting for you when you do!

Record what you experience in your journal before moving on to the next chapter.

Exercise Four – Grounding

Step One: Set a timer for five minutes. Prepare your toothbrush with toothpaste. Feel your feet on the floor as you stand in a comfortable position.

Step Two: Close your eyes and focus on your breath. Don't try to change it. Just notice what happens as you bring your attention to your breath for a couple of breaths.

Step Three: Bring your breath gently into your torso and down into your belly. Perform a few full torso breaths, feeling your breath filling your abdominal and chest cavities, and then release the breath completely.

Step Four: As you breathe into your belly, imagine the breath travelling down your legs and your arms. As you breathe out, empty your lungs completely by exhaling through your mouth. Do this a few times.

Step Five: As you breathe into your belly, feel the breath travelling all the way down into your feet and into your hands. Imagine the breath bathing the soles of your feet and your palms. As you breathe out, imagine the breath releasing through the tips of your toes and your fingers. Do this for the remainder of the time.

Step Six: When the time is up, slowly open your eyes. Take a moment to appreciate the experience that focused breathing creates.

Exercise Five – Mindful Tooth Brushing

Step One: Set a timer for two minutes. Feel your feet on the floor and feel your hands by your side as you stand in a comfortable position.

Step Two: Pick up the toothbrush and begin to brush your teeth. Use every sense available to you as you brush your teeth. What do you feel, see, smell, hear and taste? What do you intuitively sense?

Step Three: Move slowly around your mouth. Notice what you experience as you clean each tooth and the gums in which they sit. Finish by brushing the roof of your mouth and your tongue.

Step Four: When you've finished brushing your teeth, examine your teeth and your mouth. Notice what you experience.

What did you notice? What effect did attentively brushing your teeth have on your thoughts? Your emotional state? Your physical state? The actions you chose to take in brushing your teeth?

What was it like to bring mindfulness to a normal, everyday activity? What's the experience of your teeth and your mouth now that you've brought your full attention to the activity? Don't forget to notice how your teeth and mouth feel, and write what you observe in your journal.

Taking Appropriate Action

When you bring your full attention to any activity you perform, you notice things that you don't notice when you do it mindlessly. Were there any sore spots? Were you inclined to take further action?

When you bring your full attention to an activity or experience, you are better equipped to take appropriate action. Often you notice things that would otherwise pass you by.

Why is this important? Think about your physical health. Think about the health of your relationships. Think about the quality of your work. Can you see that bringing your full attention to any activity you do creates the opportunity to manage things in a complete way?

Say, for example, you have to complete a weekly status report for your team. Imagine what it would be like to activate a mindful state before you complete the report. Write down what comes up.

Record what you imagine, but don't stop there. I invite you to experiment by actually doing it. What might you discover?

Sometimes the mere act of appreciation goes a long way. You might, for example, value the function your teeth provide for you every day. You could discover the value that taking care of them attentively could bring to you.

You might start to see the value in completing a weekly report that previously irritated you. You might even start to enjoy acknowledging yourself for the results you produced that week.

There are an endless number of things you could discover, and your discoveries will be unique to you. The discovery does not have to look and feel a certain way at all. The important thing to recognise is that the act of discovery brings you a fuller picture of the reality you're exploring, whether it's your teeth or the weekly action report.

Imagine what your life would be like if you spent your days in the office, at home with your children or on the squash court with a similar degree of focus and attention on yourself and your relationship to your environment.

It may seem impossible to imagine, but it is absolutely possible to do. And you do not miss a trick when you develop this kind of awareness. Now, how useful would that be in life? Very useful indeed!

Let me share with you an example of what it can make possible in reality.

I met an extreme runner who regularly ran distances of up to 200 miles in under 48 hours.

I know. It sounds impossible, right?

I asked him what he was thinking as he was on mile 140. His partner said, "Just get to the end." He corrected her by saying, "I'm actually checking in with my heart, lungs, back, legs and feet, making micro adjustments to ensure my body is working at an optimal level."

This illustrates a key purpose of mindfulness. Giving his full attention to his body enables him to work with his body. It means he can run for miles without stopping. Most people can't imagine running 26 miles, never mind 200!

Mindfulness enables you to respond to life from a fuller level of consciousness in the present moment. You stop being a slave to survival-based thinking, and you start becoming a master of your performance in life. You discover what you're really capable of, and it's much more than your survival mind will allow you to imagine.

See if you can bring a similar degree of mindfulness to the process of writing as you record what you are discovering in your journal. Notice what happens as you do.

Let's give your body a voice.

Chapter 7

Giving the Body a Voice

Hopefully you've located your mindfulness muscle, and you've started to develop it now. How has it helped you?

Take a moment to recognise how this muscle is being activated within you. Ask yourself:

- What have I gained from bringing mindfulness to routine tasks?
- What tasks benefitted from mindfulness being brought to them?
- What other benefits have I already gained by practising mindfulness?
- Where and how will I expand my practice of mindfulness?

The results may or may not be dramatic. Sometimes you have a big 'a-ha' moment that transforms your worldview.

At other times, it may seem like nothing is happening. This is typical. Stick with it.

Like any skill, there are moments when it seems there's nothing happening. Once you've begun to exercise the muscle of mindfulness, you'll need to keep up the practice and continue to challenge yourself by expanding your application of it.

Mastering mindfulness is a little like brushing your teeth. It would be great if you could do the job once, and then it's accomplished forever. This is not how life works, and it's not how mindfulness works. I would argue that life would be very unsatisfying if all tasks were that one-dimensional. Investigate what it is like to observe yourself fully as you undertake even the most mundane task. Prepare to be surprised and delighted by what you discover.

How has bringing mindfulness to your life affected your ability to respond rather than react to situations?

Responsiveness Enables Prevention

Let's review responding and reacting within the context of brushing your teeth. Did you notice any places where your teeth or gums might have needed some special attention? Think how reacting rather than responding to this mindful discovery would have looked.

If you reacted, you might have winced in pain and vowed to avoid a particular part of your mouth, or you might have brushed your teeth with greater force to remove the build-up of coffee stains. While these reactions are understandable, they would not address the underlying source of pains and stains, and vigorous brushing, for example, can cause more problems than it solves, defeating the object of the exercise.

What might responding look like? How does it fit with the promise that led you to clean your teeth?

When you brush your teeth, you might recognise all sorts of promises: you want to keep your mouth healthy; you want to avoid bad breath; you want to maintain a winning smile of sparkly white teeth.

Maybe you do it as a promise to your mother, who reminded you to clean your teeth morning and night for years. Each promise will provide a context for your action of brushing your teeth.

As you carry out your usual routine, you discover that despite your efforts something is not quite working or could work better. Responding looks like investigating further to find out if there are different actions you could take to improve the health of your mouth or the dazzling whiteness of your smile. You might promise to expand your set of actions, like booking a dentist appointment, flossing, using a whitening toothpaste or cutting back on coffee, to remedy the problem.

Which approach is most likely to create the result you really want? Responding!

How does mindfulness support you to be responsive, rather than reactive? When you are aware of the situation you are addressing, you can detect what is not working early on. Respond rather than react to messages you receive, and you are empowered to take appropriate action to achieve the expanded result.

Prevention is better than cure. Respond rather than react and you can correct something quickly, more easily and with greater effect than if you leave it unchecked.

The Power of Observation

Mindfulness expands your observational skills by bringing a state of relaxation to your body. Slow, deliberate breathing activates the parasympathetic nervous system, which takes control when you are at rest. It allows your entire body, including your eyes, ears and brain, to soften, open up and expand.

People with busy or stress-filled lives can find their sympathetic nervous system stuck in a loop. Adrenaline and cortisol surge through your bloodstream in response to a real or perceived threat. Everything constricts and all energy reserves coalesce in service to survival.

Shallow breathing is one sign your sympathetic nervous system is running the show. This gets as much oxygen into your body as quickly as possible but too much shallow breathing, combined with stress-induced hypervigilance, can set off uncomfortable reactions like panic attacks.

Our bodies evolved to kick off this process in an emergency, to help us fight, flee, freeze or fawn in the face of danger. But, stress-filled lives can trigger the sympathetic nervous system, making every challenge occur as an emergency.

Mindfulness brings your attention to your breath, helping you to relax and let go of the intensity of a survival-based approach to life. This is when your body functions at its best.

Can you see how your body is communicating with you all the time? I hope so.

Our bodies share messages with us in many ways. You might associate your body's communication with pleasure and pain. I want to introduce you to a new realm of physiological communication - vibration.

Vibration is movement of some kind. It can come in many forms, but there are three key forms you will explore when working with your body:

- Light (colour and image)
- Sound
- Sensation.

Mindfulness lets you receive and process the vibratory signals your body is sending. In fact, you already know this to be true.

Consider your own use of language. Are you familiar with phrases that describe a physical sensation with a visual or audial metaphor?

For example, if you suffer from headaches, it's common to describe the pain as a nail being driven through your skull or a vice gripping your temples. When we're happy, it's common to describe the experience as the heart singing.

It's a way of communicating an experience to a variety of processing centres in the brain. Using different parts of your brain helps you solve problems because you are examining them from different perspectives. You already do it. You were just not aware of it until now.

Let's play with this as a possibility. I don't want you to just believe what I say. I want you to experience what I'm suggesting. It's through your experiencing that you get to own mindfulness as a way of being for yourself.

Once you've practised this exercise, write what you discover in your journal.

Exercise Six – Listening to the Body Speak

Step One: Set a timer for five minutes. Sit in a chair with your feet on the ground, arms and legs uncrossed, back straight, chin straight and body relaxed. Take a few deep torso breaths in and out and then take yourself through the full-body relaxation exercise so you are fully connected.

Step Two: Scan your body with your mind and notice if a certain area of the body calls for attention. Lightly place your attention on this part of the body.

Step Three: Notice what comes up as you place your attention on this part of the body. What you notice could be an image that illustrates the sensation. You could hear a sound or a voice as if your body wants to show you something or is speaking to you. You might notice another sensation. You might see a colour. You might notice nothing at all.

It is important to allow whatever happens to happen. You may have to practise this part of the exercise a few times until you learn the language of your body. Everyone is different. Your relationship with your body will be yours and yours alone, and it will evolve as you become more related to your body.

Step Four: When you've established a clear communication link with your body, ask what it would like from you in this moment.

Notice what message you receive.

Notice the way your body chooses to communicate with you.

Notice if there's an action you can take immediately, if there's an action you can take when you open your eyes, or if there's a series of actions you can take to address your body's request.

Step Five: Gently direct your breath to that part of the body. As you breathe in, imagine that part of your body being bathed in the vibration of the breath. As you breathe out, imagine the breath moving through the area of focus and leaving your body. Notice the impact this has on you.

Step Six: When the time is up, thank your body for being willing to enter into dialogue with you, bring your attention back to your breath from the chest and slowly open your eyes.

What did you notice? What effect did directing your breath to this part of your body have on your thoughts? Your emotional state? Your physical state? Your experience of life itself?

What was it like to bring mindfulness to a part of your body to deal with its state of being? What effect did your breath have on the part of your body that requested your attention?

Mindfulness's Role in Self-Care

I put these exercises into action all the time. In fact, as I wrote this exercise, I stopped to breathe into my neck and shoulders. You know how working at a computer for a long time puts a strain on your body?

As I began to breathe into my neck and shoulders, I saw an image of head rolls, and thought, 'That's what I need!' So, I began to bring my attention to my neck and shoulders with slow head rolls going in both directions.

Listening to my body in the moment means that I can continue to write with no pain. At the same time, I know that my body is reaching its limit of being willing to support me while sitting at the computer. I am committed to my promise to take care of my body. By responding to its call to do something else, I take action to provide my body with essentials that will ensure I can sit at the computer tomorrow.

In taking care of your body, you take care of your mind. You create the conditions that enable your mind to move your body to create the things you want to create. In my case right now, it's a page full of what I hope are useful, guiding words. In your case, it might be your 100th flower bouquet, another mile on the bicycle or an A* grade in an exam.

Your body and mind work best when they work together, however much science tries to carve distinctions between the two.

Uniting them in support of each other helps you to accomplish what you want to accomplish.

Accomplishment brings feelings of fulfilment to most people. I'm sure that is what you want for yourself, and I hope it's clear that feeling fulfilled through accomplishment is what I want for you.

Your breath provides a critical link in the chain of accomplishment. It rounds out the experience. It helps you become aware of the whole experience. It expands your insight into what fuels your performance and ultimately your accomplishments.

This helps you repeat, augment and master what works. By slowing down and turning within, it increases your ability to bring agility into your own personal performance. Isn't that worth having?

Let's now add some colour to your body's language.

Chapter 8

Adding Colour to Your Body's Language

Reflect upon the new relationship you are developing with your body. What has it been telling you? Have you listened and acted on its guidance or dismissed it as nonsense?

Wherever you are, it is perfectly normal and there is more to gain if you explore and test this notion of relating to your body in a new way. In particular, you stand to elevate your performance by working smart, not hard. Doesn't that sound appealing?

If you haven't already, my hope for you is that you will allow yourself to experiment. I am opening a door. You can take the opportunity to discover and create what works for you.

Are you in need of a bit of inspiration? Here's a story that will help you understand the power of what I am guiding you to explore.

My husband and I were trekking in South America. It was the last day of a four-day trek, and our destination was the *pièce de résistance,* a glacier. But my heels were covered in blisters, and as we set off, I thought I was going to have to abandon the hike. The blisters were hurting so badly it felt as though my heels were being pricked with thousands of tiny needles.

Notice the imagery I use to describe the pain?

At the point I was about to give up, I decided to put this theory to the test. I started to talk to my feet. I said, 'Feet, I am so sorry you are hurting. If you need me to turn around now, I will. I just want to tell you how grateful I am for everything you do for me, and I realise I never express my gratitude to you. I am telling you now, and I will do whatever it takes to look after you.'

Here's what happened. Within moments, I forgot about the pain. A few hours into the hike, I discovered that this was the most challenging trail of all four days and yet I clambered over tree trunks and gullies like I had walked this path many times in my life. We got to the glacier and back to the camp in record time, and I hardly noticed the blisters for the rest of the holiday.

That is the effect you can have on your body and your life when you make a conscious effort to acknowledge the messages your body is sending you and consciously connect and communicate with it in return.

When you consider my story, do you detect a certain character to the words, as if they were sprinkled with a specific spice or coloured with a particular shade? They certainly have a definite tone to them, don't they?

How would you describe the tone?

For example, what emotion do you hear and feel is being expressed by my feet? Then, what emotion do you hear and feel is being expressed through my words?

What effect did my words have on my feet and subsequently my experience of that day's trek?

To be honest, I was as surprised by the result as you may be but from that moment on, I have related to my body in an entirely new way. I appreciate the messages it is sending. I listen, I enquire into the source of the problem and I collaborate with my body to alleviate pain and discomfort and acknowledge the pleasure it enables me to feel.

The last bit, the acknowledgement, is important. It is something we forget to do, and yet gratitude and appreciation cure a wealth of ailments: physical, emotional, psychological and spiritual.

Do You Dominate or Collaborate?

Have you noticed that this is not the usual way of doing things? What is unusual about it?

'Mind over matter' is a well-worn phrase. It suggests a hierarchical relationship in which the mind dominates the body. This might feel familiar, especially when you relate to your body with scorn or frustration: criticising lumps and bumps here, expressing annoyance at its lack of cooperation there.

Even when you do something that you think is good for your body, like exercising or eating well, consider the energy, specifically the emotion, that fuels these actions. Do you treat your body with contempt, like a slave, or do you treat it with respect, like a friend?

Imagine treating your body as your beloved, deserving of the highest care and attention. How would your relationship with your body change? How would the state of your body change?

I am not perfect at this. I don't think there is a perfect way. We live busy lives that make it challenging to be perfectly attentive to our bodies. And let's be clear. I don't mean spending a fortune on therapists to 'treat' your body, either. Here's a picture of what I do: I apologise to my body when I have done something that doesn't suit it, like eating the wrong foods or injuring it by overexercising. I thank my body when it has been willing to help me perform an important task. I seek help from health experts when necessary to support its healing.

Here's the thing. Words hold power, even as thoughts. If you want to be a powerful force for good in a relationship, you choose your words carefully to produce the best outcome. The same is true for your body. If you relate to your body in a supportive way, your body will respond by supporting you.

There is a misconception that consciousness lies only in your brain. Actually, your entire body holds consciousness: emotion and memory reside wherever you have living cells. Connecting with your body provides a fast route to the source of what you're feeling and why you're feeling it, whether it's a difficult emotion like anger or sadness or a physiological response like a churning stomach or a tight throat.

Where does it all begin? In the mind, of course, but the mind is not always the easiest place to start, especially when you are dealing with issues that happened long ago and have since been filed away in the unconscious.

Here's how it really works. You have a thought. The thought generates an emotion. The emotion generates a sensation. The sensation generates an impulse. The impulse generates an attitude. The attitude drives the action. The action becomes a behaviour. The behaviour generates a result.

Now, you can deconstruct this at any point along the route from thought to result. The result, either inside or outside, is the easiest point to identify.

Perhaps you have a recurring problem, persistent colds, for example. Is the problem the persistent colds or feeling unhappy that you are getting persistent colds? What do you do to get to the root of your challenged immune system?

Being unhappy about the problem is a natural response, but it will not necessarily motivate you to take action. It does, however, give you a clue that underneath the physical symptom lies a thought about it.

And consider that this thought may be the thing that has the cold keep occurring. Do you see yourself as a victim of the big, bad cold virus? Do you berate your body for being unable to fight it off?

Work your way back to discover the original thought that kicked off the initial chain of events, in particular the emotional response to the physical symptoms of a cold. You will start to notice that it gets activated the moment the first signs of a cold start, or maybe even from the moment someone around you sneezes.

If you can recognise the thought that accompanies the experience we call a 'cold,' you have the power to change the thought and take a new set of actions to deal with the cold. It could be that you take a remedy to boost your immune system, like Vitamin C or echinacea. You could examine your life leading up to the cold to see what could have compromised your immunity.

In short, you have greater access to taking new actions that will create new outcomes. This gives you the power to elevate your performance to new heights. Otherwise, chances are you'll continue to create the same results you've always created. That's not necessarily bad. It's just not going to support you to improve your performance.

Where Does It all Begin?

It all begins with a thought.

The best way of discovering your habitual thoughts is to work backwards, step by step. You can see it as a process of reverse engineering the result to its source.

If you decide you want to produce a different result, what do you need to change? Your thoughts! If you attempt to change anything other than the thought, you might make small strides, but you won't make the changes you desire, and they will only be temporary.

This might sound daunting, but the truth is it's easier than you think. Sometimes the smallest tweak in thinking can make a massive difference to your performance.

What role do emotions play? Emotions provide the fuel that brings the result into manifestation. They link the thought with your physiology and actions, which translate into behaviours that produce results. Emotions carry bucketloads of energy that serve or thwart your results, depending upon how skilfully you handle them.

Let's take the example of a cold. When you feel the signs of a cold coming on, what's your first thought? What's the corresponding emotion to that thought? What sensations arise in your body? Bear in mind these sensations may be different from cold symptoms.

What impulses arise? What attitude do you adopt? What actions do you take? What behaviours do you adopt? What results do you produce?

If you can't recognise the thought instantly, work backwards. What are the inevitable results based on your usual behaviour? What actions make up that behavioural pattern? What attitude drives these actions and behaviours? What impulse lies beneath the attitude? What sensations generated the impulse? What emotions fuelled the sensations? What thought or thoughts instigated the emotion?

What I am doing here is providing you with an experience of my trademarked methodology called I-AM-I. Standing for Intentional Applied Mindfulness Integration, its primary purpose is to re-engineer neural pathways.

To re-engineer anything, you must break it down from its current state into its component parts until you reach the activating source. In the case of neural pathways, it is usually a thought, maybe an image, memory or symbol and a story or narrative about the original thought.

Once you reach the point of origin, you can examine it to understand the impact it is having on your life. At that point, you can choose to keep it or discard it and create new thoughts that create new pathways, but you have to begin by first acknowledging the presence of the existing pathway.

When you understand how neural pathways work, you can respond to rather than react from them. The trick is knowing of their existence in the first place. Applying mindfulness using a methodology like I-AM-I to intentionally re-engineer and integrate neural pathways gives you a level of mastery in working with your neurology.

Pretty cool, isn't it?

I do not expect you to become an expert at this just by reading this book. It takes a lot of practice to be able to do this for yourself, and it makes a huge difference to work with an expert, like a coach or therapist, who can help you deconstruct and reconstruct these pathways. What I will do is outline the process at other times in the book so you can see how to apply it, step by step.

At this point, I want to say something briefly about the vibrational phenomenon we call emotion.

People become attached to feeling emotion, placing a high degree of emphasis on the importance of emotional expression. In my experience, it's a hangover from the days when catharsis served as a popular route to emotional healing. Do you remember the band Primal Scream or the Tears for Fears song, Shout? They both drew inspiration from primal scream therapy, a trendy 1970s approach to emotional release.

Let me be clear. I am not undermining the approach. Expressing emotion has its place in the healing process. However, catharsis without applying responsible, accountable and intentional mindful reflection and integration is just emoting. The cycle perpetuates: people express the emotion without knowing its origin, continuing to feed the thoughts that produce the emotion, or they attempt to suppress the emotion altogether. Neither approach will free you from an unproductive emotional roundabout.

View emotions as one layer of many that provide valuable information to you about yourself. They are no more or less important than any other link in the chain, but they must be regarded, not ignored, to be of use. When used skilfully, they can be very powerful tools.

Through mindfulness, you will become more acquainted with your emotional self. Emotional literacy is shockingly absent from our everyday vocabulary, and yet emotions contain energy that can be harnessed and put to good use. Certain environments like business settings typically shy away from emotional expression, seeing emotions as disruptors of rational thought.

Experiencing real emotion is what distinguishes human beings from robots; robots are capable of mimicking emotions, good at detecting them, able to communicate them but entirely unable to feel them. Why? Emotions are a function of biology.

I invite you to discover something new about your emotional self, this time from a place of mindfulness. It's typical to fear being overwhelmed by emotion when you enter unexplored territory. Your impulse might be to retain control. I get it!

The benefits of exploring emotions through mindfulness is that the state of mindfulness creates a sturdy, safe container in which to examine potentially challenging aspects of yourself, such as unconscious thoughts, emotions, impulses and physiological reactions. In being fully present in your body, you 'contain' the vibration that emotions generate, enabling you to explore them without unwanted, messy spillage.

Let's explore your emotional self through an exercise. Like all exercises, complete this in full and record what you experience in your journal.

Exercise Seven – Allowing Your Body To Express Itself

Step One: Set a timer for 10 minutes. Sit in a chair with your feet on the ground, arms and legs uncrossed, back straight and body relaxed. Take a few deep breaths in and out and then take yourself through the full-body relaxation exercise so you are connected and grounded.

Step Two: Allow your attention to be drawn to something. It could be a thought. It could be a sensation. It could be an obvious emotion. Notice what it is.

Step Three: Notice all the information that comes with it. What are you thinking? What images are emerging? What emotions are you feeling? What bodily sensations are you having? What impulses do you notice? What attitudes are arising? What actions are you inclined to take? What behaviours are becoming apparent?

Step Four: See if you can allow the information, including thoughts, images, emotions, sensations, impulses, attitudes, actions and behaviours, to just be there without having to do anything. Notice what happens.

Step Five: Direct your breath softly and gently to a particular part of your body. If you are having a recurring thought, direct your breath to the spot where that thought is emanating. If you have an emotional experience, direct the breath to the spot where the emotion is emanating. Direct your breath to this spot as you breathe in and see the breath leaving through the area as you breathe out, taking the thought, emotion, sensation, impulse, image, attitude, action or behaviour with it. When it feels complete, notice if any new thoughts, emotions, sensations, impulses, attitudes, actions and behaviours come to mind.

Step Six: When the time is up, take three deep breaths, in through the nose and out through the mouth, and slowly open your eyes. Spend a moment scanning your body and your awareness, just noticing what is present for you. Take some time to record what you discovered in your journal.

What did you notice? What effect did directing your breath to this part of your body have on your thoughts? Your emotional state? Your physical state? Your experience of life itself?

Re-Engineering Your Experiences

What was it like to use mindfulness to re-engineer your thoughts, feelings and emotions? What result were you able to produce as you completed the exercise?

Consider your emotions as the artist's palette from which you paint your life. Recognising their role in producing the kind of results you want in life and being responsible for your emotional self gives you a considerable amount of freedom and power.

If you were to paint your emotional life on a canvas, how might it look right now? What colours would you choose? What images would typify a scene from your life? What experience would it evoke in others? What's your response to it?

Here is the best bit. You are at the source of every piece of artwork you create. You have choice and the power necessary to invent new levels of performance in your life. Mindfulness enables you to tap into and harness your inner resources to accomplish your goals, which further feeds and expands your inner resources. It's a virtuous circle.

So, what do you want to create?

Chapter 9

Uncovering the Source of Your Emotions

The contents of the mind are a mystery to most people, yet when examined, it becomes apparent that the mind, specifically thought, is the source of everything you experience in the world.

Human beings like to distinguish things and separate them out. This useful work helps us identify the role of each component that makes up the whole. Problems arise when we assume that these parts operate in isolation.

The truth is, everything is connected and integrated. That includes your mind, your emotions and your body, all of which are inextricably linked. Mindfulness helps you integrate these components into a high performance working whole.

The Physiology of Emotions

Take emotions, for example. When you have a thought that generates fear, your adrenal glands emit adrenaline and cortisol, what I call the 'survival hormones'. Adrenaline and cortisol mobilise the body for survival by galvanising the sympathetic nervous system, directing your body, emotions and mind to focus on dealing with the perceived threat. In a healthy organic system, the body shakes off the survival hormones, the emotions stabilise and the mind lets go of the fearful thoughts once the threat disappears. The parasympathetic nervous system activates, returning the organism to a state of rest.

This process is particularly evident in animals that live in the wild. Think of an antelope, a creature preyed upon by several predators. They stand on alert when they sense a threat, ready at a moment's notice to fight, flee, freeze or fawn, depending upon the situation. When they are certain the threat has vanished, their bodies shake from head to tail. They are literally shaking off the effects of the survival hormones and returning to a state of relaxation. [9]

Expectant and new parents are keenly aware of the presence of oxytocin, the love hormone, that mothers excrete as they breastfeed their babies. Oxytocin facilitates the essential bonding that generates intense feelings of love and a desire to nurture and protect their utterly dependent infant. While breastfeeding certainly promotes bonding, fathers or partners who participate in the feeding and nurturing process while their infants are young also enjoy the effects of oxytocin.

Oxytocin affects the animal kingdom, too. You may have seen the videos of cats mothering orphaned rabbits and ducklings, or even tigers raising piglets. These remarkable pairings may seem rare, but they do happen, more often than you realise. The release of oxytocin, usually experienced around the heart centre, makes it possible for love between even the most unlikely of pairs.

Traumatic situations, like very traumatic birth experiences, can stymie the natural flow of the oxytocin hormone. This can significantly limit a parent's ability to create the essential bond with their child, making the early weeks and months of parenting a challenge. The good news: it is always possible to generate love for an infant. The way to do it is to heal the trauma and its effects on the bond between parent and child.

Speaking of trauma, what is it about a situation that creates the experience of trauma? Why is it that the same event will deeply wound one person, while another person can shrug it off?

Health, including mental health, obviously begins in the mind, and it comes about as a direct result of the meaning you give to a situation. Alfred Adler, a contemporary of

Freud, asserted that trauma is kept alive through the stories we tell ourselves and others about a given event, not the event itself. [10]

How does this work in reality? A client suffering extreme post-natal PTSD (post-traumatic stress disorder) found herself completely healed from her experience in one session. How did she accomplish this? I helped her recreate her story from one of being a victim of an insensitive medical team to acknowledging that, despite the challenging circumstances, the team saved both her and her baby from certain death. This realisation helped her accept her less-than-ideal birthing experience and allowed her to be the brilliant mother she longed to be.

It's easy to believe that you are at the mercy of your biology. It's easy to blame your past experiences for your current situation. Yes, there are genetic components to health and yes, we all have experiences that challenge us.

However, even hereditary challenges can be met and overcome with the right application of mental processes. The state of your health is determined by the thoughts you have about a situation and the chain of events that these thoughts initiate.

Can you see now why it's so important to performance for you to be mindful? So, why aren't you familiar with the fullness of your mind?

Until recent years psychology has been widely discredited as a pseudoscience. The tin-foil-hat-wearing conspiracy realist in me recognises that it's convenient for you to remain ignorant of the way your neurology works. It means it can be used against you, and it often is. Think about sales tactics or coercive political campaigns designed to steer you in a certain direction. It's easy to manipulate people when they are not in control of the fullness of the mind, hence the need for mindfulness.

According to *Wiley Psychology Updates,* your brain processes over 6,000 thoughts per day, and a large percentage of those thoughts are negative. [11]

Most of these thoughts occur without your conscious knowledge. They run on autopilot in the background.

Couple this with the fact that thought is the source of all emotion. Emotions don't spring from nowhere. They arise as the result of a thought or series of thoughts that trigger a physiological and emotional reaction in you. The reaction you experience is the direct result of the meaning you have created with your thoughts.

If your thoughts generate feelings that you enjoy, like passion or enthusiasm or love, you will probably want to continue to think what you think. However, if your thoughts are generating feelings that you find uncomfortable, like anger or worry or depression, you may want to change your thinking.

As I described earlier, emotions have a physiological component. Fear activates the adrenal glands, preparing your body to react to danger, real or imagined, through the fight, flight, freeze or fawn reaction. Your body produces oxytocin when you experience feelings of love for another human being. A lack of serotonin in the brain's neuroreceptors may be linked to depression whereas dopamine is associated with the experience of pleasure and can be linked to addictions.

While I could go into more depth here, there are many books and free resources online if you want to explore this aspect of your physiology further. New advances in neurological understanding are being made all the time. It's an exciting field of study, and it would be of great benefit to you to understand the interplay between the neurological and endocrine systems.

For our purposes, what I invite you to understand and experience for yourself is that the mind, the body and the emotions are inextricably linked. Your experience at any of these levels provides a window into what you are experiencing at other levels.

The Mindful Game of Tennis

Take, for instance, a minor sporting injury like tennis elbow. Though tennis elbow will not kill you, it will stop you from playing sports like tennis or golf at your peak. If your idea of taking care of yourself means a few hours on the court or striding around a tree-lined golf course for 18 holes, and you get tennis elbow, you'll probably have some associated thoughts and feelings about it.

I know I did. I love tennis, but I hadn't really played in years. I enrolled in a tennis course at my local club. Within about three weeks, I felt pain in my right elbow like I had never experienced before. It took weeks to heal and, while I used pain relief and a brace to minimise further damage, it put a damper on my plans to spend lots of time chasing a yellow ball around a court.

Tennis is a game I love, and it's a great way for me to get exercise. I felt defeated that my attempts to be healthy were thwarted. I noticed all sorts of conversations arising about my age, and the frustration that my body wouldn't do at 50-something what it would at 30-something. I tried to push through and soldier on.

Did any of this help? Not a bit. In fact, it only made the tennis elbow worse.

So, taking my own advice, I started loving my elbow by soaking my arm in Epsom salts on a regular basis. I learned some stretches for my wrists and elbow that I could do before and after a tennis session. I cut down on the play while it was at its worst and did strengthening exercises for the muscles in my arms to manage the tension in the tendons. I got regular massages from a masseuse who worked on my hands, wrists and arms with soothing, healing oils.

Now, I recognise that sitting at a computer typing for hours at a time contributes to the tension in my wrists and arms, so I stop periodically to stretch. It hadn't occurred to me that my work may be impacting my leisure time and my health in such a direct way. Once I stopped complaining about it and started to take positive action to help myself and my elbow, the pain began to subside.

Has this approach helped? Immensely. I am not playing as much tennis as I'd like, but in being flexible and creative in my approach, and being committed to taking care of my elbow, I have discovered other routes to my goal. For example, playing table tennis with my son, which needs less arm strength, is almost as satisfying. Not quite, but almost.

If you accept that your mind, emotions and body are linked, then you accept that a thought contributed to an emotion that contributed to either the creation or the perpetuation of something. However, you might be unaware of these thoughts and the accompanying emotion. What's your tennis elbow? What's your route to discovering the thoughts and emotions that may be getting in your way in the important areas of your life?

Retrieving the Files of Experience

You see, what I discovered in my exploration of the thoughts around my tennis elbow was a deeply held belief that I would never be able to accomplish what I wanted to accomplish. This started at age ten, when I had to stop taking dance lessons, which was the best part of my week. My dreams of being a dancer on Broadway died when my dance teachers stopped teaching in my town. Living in a small town in 1970s Tennessee didn't provide many opportunities to pursue a career on Broadway. Banjo picking and country singing, perhaps, but not Broadway dancing.

When I really started to look, I discovered that the thought that I would never be able to accomplish what I wanted to accomplish generated thoughts of being defeated, which generated the emotion of hopelessness. And this blackness influenced my whole life. Being a generally positive person, this realisation shocked me. Many times, through sheer force of will, I overcame it, but often at a cost to me or to others. Getting to this layer of mindful experience has enabled me to discard this belief and create a new one; that I am fulfilling my dreams. It's what has me sitting here, writing this book. Who knows? With that kind of attitude, I may dance on Broadway yet!

Remember that you think 6,000 thoughts per day. Some of these thoughts lie in the hippocampus, which is the part of the brain that stores memories and the accompanying thoughts about the memories. It's the filing cabinet of every experience you have ever experienced in your body.

Imagine trying to be conscious of that all the time. It's mind-boggling just thinking about it!

These filed memories come to your attention when they get triggered by familiar situations, launching a chain of events that influence your thoughts, emotions and physiological responses, which drive your behavioural choices.

Have you ever recognised that you repeat certain patterns of behaviour over and over again, seemingly inexplicably? Now you know why.

It's fine if you trigger patterns that generate the experience of satisfaction, accomplishment and fulfilment, but it's not so great if you replay experiences of failure, resignation or powerlessness.

It's a useful exercise to examine situations of both types to help you see how this works. Let's apply my I-AM-I neural pathway re-engineering process to a physical experience to see if you can uncover the source of the experience.

Exercise Eight: Re-Engineering an Experience

Step One: Set a timer for 10 minutes. Sit in a chair with your feet on the ground, arms and legs uncrossed, back straight and body relaxed. Take a few deep breaths in and out and then take yourself through the full-body relaxation exercise so you are connected and grounded.

Step Two: Take your attention to a sensation in your body, preferably one that is recurring like tightness in the shoulders or pain in your knee. It could be anywhere in your body and you could experience the sensation as pleasure or pain.

Step Three: Take a few deep breaths and notice if there is any emotion associated with the sensation that arises. If you can't access emotion immediately, see what else you notice. Perhaps you see an image or you feel an impulse to act. Just notice.

Step Four: Ask your consciousness to show you a memory associated with this sensation. Allow yourself to recall the memory as fully as possible. As you recall the memory, notice what it brings up for you. What emotions do you feel? What thoughts are you thinking? What meaning is associated with the memory? What impact did the experience the memory represents have on you then? What impact is it having on you now? Allow whatever is present to be there. If deep, unsettling emotions arise, take a few deep breaths into your belly and down into your arms and legs, allowing the emotional vibration to release from your body as you breathe out through your mouth.

Step Five: When you're ready, ask yourself what new information you are noticing by revisiting this experience. Perhaps there are new thoughts you can have, new actions you can take and new ways you can feel that will support you in your life going forward. When the process comes to its natural conclusion, thank your body for being your partner in helping you live your life fully and freely.

Step Six: When the time is up, take a few deep breaths in through the nose and out through the mouth, and slowly open your eyes. Sit for a moment to bathe in the experience, gather your thoughts and integrate the experience.

What did you notice? What effect did re-engineering a sensation have on your ability to get to the source of your recurrent physical experience?

In particular, notice the new information that arises as you revisit a familiar experience. Notice how your thoughts expand and change as you bring a new-found perspective to an old experience. Notice the impact this new perspective creates for you in the moment. Finally, speculate on how this new perspective will affect your performance from this point forward.

Discovering the Power of Mindfulness

Are you beginning to see just how powerful this mindfulness work is? It enables you to control the effect life has on you rather than having life affect you.

True power looks like the ability to be master of your performance, including the outcomes. When you're able to master performance, you're able to master life. Isn't that exciting?

Here's how it works in reality.

A client of mine, a young person, was facing an important set of academic exams. Two factors made the exams particularly scary for him: his learning disability and his previous academic performance. His school had decided that he had to attain a certain result or he would not be invited back for senior school.

As he shared his story, I heard him say many times, "I can't do it." So, I asked him to hold out his hand, spread his fingers, cover his face and look at the paper on his desk saying to himself, "I can't do it." His hand represented the limiting belief that was clouding his ability to see things clearly, so of course he couldn't do it.

I asked him to breathe deeply, remove his hand and notice what he experienced. The words that immediately came to him were, "Maybe I can do it."

You'll be pleased to know that, not only did he get the grades needed to stay in school, but he has now graduated from university and has landed a brilliant job. Being open to the possibility that he could do it gave him the intrinsic motivation he needed to make it happen.

I hope you realise that these are the extraordinary benefits of mindfulness that are misunderstood and therefore missed. It gets shoved into the corner of being merely a relaxation tool. There's nothing wrong with that per se. It's just that mindfulness, when applied insightfully, can positively influence the course of a person's life. It enables you to connect with yourself and make choices that power conscious, intentional, mindful, expanded performance. When you hold the power of mindful performance in your grasp, you also hold the power of brilliant performance in your grasp.

Now that you're acquainted with the true nature of mindfulness, it's time to put some of what you've learned into practice. It's quite probable that you're doing this already. I certainly hope so!

Some of the exercises you have learned may be more appropriate to complete initially at home. Once you get the hang of them, you'll be able to complete these processes anywhere. There are ways you can bring mindfulness to any aspect of your life *in the moment it's needed*, and I will guide you through a few examples of how to do that.

Chapter 10

Applying Mindfulness to Improve Performance

Take a moment to reflect on what you've accomplished so far by discovering the power and the benefits of mindfulness and how this might be used to improve performance.

What have you discovered? What changes have you noticed? Where have you noticed those changes? What impact are the exercises having on your experience of yourself?

You've learned how to connect with yourself on several different levels. You've discovered how each level interconnects with the others. And you've practised skills that allow you to shift your experience from one state to another. Finally, you have opened the door to some of the hidden motivating factors behind your behaviour.

In short, you are on your way to learning the art of self-mastery.

When you think of mastery, your mind may jump to skills that are readily accessible, like playing a sport, musical instrument or chess. It seems that the action takes place primarily on the physical plane. Consider that the real work begins and continues in the mind. It is just as important to concentrate on mental acuity as it is to develop physical acuity because mental sharpness drives all other kinds of ability.

A musician friend once told me the story of his travels with a famous violinist. Travelling together on a train, my friend was struck by his companion's intense look and repetition of certain facial expressions. And then, the virtuoso's expression changed to one of calm satisfaction. When my friend asked what he had been doing, the virtuoso replied that he had been working to solve a technical problem in his performance, and he had succeeded. All the while, the violin remained in its case.

Elite sportspeople know that visualising a play over and over makes delivering the play on the pitch or the court feel natural. Sports psychology is a path well-trodden by all accomplished sports men and women who, like you and me, can indulge in unproductive, self-sabotaging thoughts and behaviours. While natural skill and enjoyment of an activity certainly help, mastery of the mind is the secret that takes professionals from being good to being great. Brilliant, even.

The same is true for any type of pursuit where participants strive for excellence. If you want to increase performance at work, at school, with your health and so on, the secret lies in being able to master the mind, specifically the content of thoughts. The idea is to train yourself to think thoughts and attitudes that produce the most beneficial emotional energy. These thoughts power and produce the ideal physical responses, which then fuel ideal behaviours, actions and ultimately results.

Think of it this way. Language is the means by which you programme yourself to think, feel and act. Language is the means by which you programme others to respond to you. Your brain acts as a receiver, picking up visual, sound, kinetic and electromagnetic vibrations and transforming them into words. It initiates an array of applications based on these words and the reactions they elicit.

The Computer: a Facsimile of the Mind

We are like computers, or rather computers and computer networks are like us. They are crude models representing the blueprint of the human nervous system and the planetary ecosystem. Unless you are an expert at computing, you probably use your devices without knowing how they work.

If you understand the basic principles of computing, you can see it as a simple representation of your nervous system. By understanding how your nervous system works, you have the power to alter the course of your entire experience of life. You become master of your own machinery.

The most basic part of your brain is the brain stem, which controls the activation of fear. Like the binary code of a computer at its most basic level, it operates on 0 and 1, 0 representing the absence of fear and 1 representing the presence of fear.

When you feel no fear, you are in a state of relaxation and your possibilities expand. Why? Because your brain is relaxed and open to exploring new ideas and possibilities.

When you feel fear your entire system gears up for survival. The survival hormones discard everything that is unnecessary for your survival, focusing your physiology and your thinking solely on maintaining your life.

On top of the 0 and 1, you have a layer of automatic processes needed to keep the machine going. Some of these, like breathing, your heartbeat, or your stomach digesting food after eating, are default settings. These settings are pretty standard for all human beings, unless you carry a genetic inheritance, experience an illness or accident or become exposed to environmental factors that alter how the processes work. Think of it as your operating system, like MS-DOS for the PC or Mac iOS.

In the main, your attention is only drawn to these processes when they are disrupted, by fear or through injury, for example.

On top of the operating system sits a series of applications that you've been creating since birth. Some are skills, like reading, writing and driving.

You need to devote a lot of time and mental, emotional and physical energy to learning a new skill. At first you feel awkward and unsure of yourself as you practise to improve your skills competency.

As your system develops and increases its capacity to handle the skill, you relax. With continued practice, you master the skill and the competency moves to the hippocampus, your memory bank. You no longer have to be conscious of your actions. This is what makes skills feel natural as if you were born with them.

Other 'applications' manifest as personality traits. These result from your interpretation of life experiences.

Remember how I explained the role that trauma plays in developing our 'personality'? Well, given that your machinery is geared towards survival, every application created from a strong survival theme, such as fear, becomes a powerful aspect of your personality. So, your high performance mindset may be less of a personal attribute of your 'soul' and more of a survival strategy.

Now, while you understand the performance benefits gained by debugging your operating system or upgrading your computer hardware and software, you might not have considered that the contents of your neural network could benefit from an upgrade, too.

Obviously, you can make changes to your hardware, or the body, but you can't trade it in for a new model. You can upgrade your software, or your programming, with the tools you have to hand right now. How? Through the language you choose to use.

Think about it. How are computers programmed? With computer programming *languages*. So, what is the function of the language you use? You programme yourself, through your thoughts, to feel the emotions that create the sensations that generate the impulses that influence the attitudes that power the actions that become behaviours that create results.

By applying mindfulness to get to know your own programming, you'll find that you can change the code, upgrade or discard applications and create new ones. Even the code entrenched and hidden from your view can be re-engineered if you take the time to listen and apply the methodology. It takes persistence and patience but it can be done.

Are you starting to get how simple this really is, that once you understand how you work, you have the power to determine how your life looks? The key is to familiarise yourself with your hardware and your software.

You cannot master the binary 0s and 1s, operating system and applications of your mind when you don't know what you're dealing with. And if you can't master your mind, you cannot align your thoughts with your emotions, sensations, impulses, attitudes, actions and behaviours to deliver the results you want for yourself. Explore mindfulness, however, and all this becomes possible.

Deconstructing the I-AM-I Process

Now that you've had a few brief encounters with my I-AM-I process, it is a good opportunity to help you understand how the process works by deconstructing it, step by step.

Let's start by looking more carefully at neural pathways. As I mentioned earlier in the book, neural pathways comprise a series of experiences that work together when triggered by something.

Let's take an example with which we're all familiar: hunger. When your stomach is empty, the nerve endings in your stomach register it and then set off a series of additional experiences. Your stomach may growl. You feel an emptiness in your abdomen. Your head might ache. You could feel tiredness or dizziness setting in. There are some experiences that are common to everyone, some that are unique to individuals and some that are dependent upon the circumstances of the hunger.

The signs of hunger may generate certain emotional reactions in you. You might notice you are quick to anger, an experience some call being 'hangry.' If you're on a diet, you might feel worried about eating too much or upset that you're finding the hunger too hard to tolerate. Perhaps you love that empty feeling in your stomach. It's possible you're enjoying the process of working up an appetite in anticipation of a special meal.

Now, in identifying the emotion above, I've also linked conscious thoughts you could be having that relate to that emotional experience, like 'eating too much' or 'anticipation of a special meal.' If you were to take time to examine these thoughts, you might find that there are underlying, or unconscious thoughts that sit just underneath the surface, acting as applications for your surface-level thoughts.

What might these thoughts be? They could be beliefs you have about hunger and food. They might be memories of being hungry and stories that accompany those memories. They could be opinions, beliefs or attitudes you have formed or acquired about food and hunger.

Are you starting to see the various points along the neural pathway? Let's outline them within the context of the example:

- Empty stomach
- Bodily behaviour and actions
- Sensations of hunger
- Emotions about hunger
- Conscious thoughts about hunger
- Unconscious thoughts about hunger.

If you're content with your relationship to hunger, and if the way you react to hunger supports your health and well-being, you may be happy to leave that application running just as it is. If not, you can *intend* to re-engineer your subconscious programming about food and hunger to enable you to improve your relationship to hunger. This, in turn, will have an impact on your performance in health and well-being.

You might be asking yourself, "How is this applicable to other areas of life?"

Great question! Let's give each bullet point its generic equivalent.

- Result
- Behaviour and action
- Sensations
- Emotions
- Conscious thoughts
- Unconscious thoughts.

Each of these points along a neural pathway can be applied to every area of performance in your life, can't they?

The way to start using this methodology is to get real about the results you are already creating. This is why data is so valuable.

Think of an area in life in which you want to improve your performance. Where would you start?

You start with the results you have already achieved in that area of life. If you check in with the reality of your results and completely accept reality as it is, you will give yourself the perfect starting point from which to re-engineer your pathways and your results.

Make sure you record what you discover in your journal so you can track your neural pathway.

- What results do you currently have? In the case of managing weight, for example, it would be what you weigh right now.

- Consider the result, and ask yourself, "What behaviours and actions am I or am I not taking to bring that result into being?"
- Consider the behaviours and actions and ask yourself, "What sensations am I feeling in my body right now as I recall these behaviours and actions?"
- Consider the sensations and ask yourself, "What emotions am I feeling in my body right now as I experience these sensations?"
- Consider the emotions and ask yourself, "What thoughts am I aware of right now that would generate these emotions?"
- Consider the thoughts and ask yourself, "What other thoughts, including memories, are fuelling these thoughts?"

Tracking back from the result to the thoughts enables you to discover the *unconscious* thoughts that influence the result. Don't worry if it's a little tough at first. It takes practice and skill to be able to sift through your own thoughts to recognise the unconscious thoughts.

What makes the difference is your ability to listen and *hear* yourself think. When you're new to mindfulness, this can be challenging, so it's important to hear your body's voice. If you want to elevate the results, work with a therapist or coach who can act as a mirror to help you identify unconscious thoughts.

When you reach the unconscious material, you will experience an emotional or cognitive release. I liken it to a splinter being extracted from your finger or foot. The extraction is painful, but when it leaves the body, there's an experience of relief and coherence that returns to bodily tissues. When you've removed the splinter, you can *intentionally apply mindfulness* to *integrate* a new neural pathway designed to support your success.

The benefits of I-AM-I can be explained this way. Removing cognitive splinters enables you to intentionally create and integrate cognitive processes and elevate coherence in cognitive functioning, making your mind work like a well-designed high performance engine.

The best way to create a new neural pathway is to take an iterative approach, refining what you create as you go along. At each point in the process, try things on before you decide to go forward with it. If something doesn't feel right, change it until it works for you. And remember to use the breath with each step!

Start with thought. Ask yourself, "What thoughts would I like to think about this area of my life?"

Then consider, "What emotions do these thoughts generate?" This is an important step. You want to ensure you use the best fuel possible to obtain the best performance. Remember that thoughts are the source of emotional fuel.

Next, ask yourself, "What sensations do these emotions generate in my body? How do I feel in my body?" If it feels good, keep going. If it doesn't, it's an indication that the thoughts you're creating need tweaking. Play with the wording until you come up with something that creates the experience of opportunity and excitement in you.

The next step is to consider, "What behaviours and actions do these thoughts, emotions and sensations compel me to take?" Notice what actions and behaviours occur as immediately obvious. Expand your actions and behaviours by inviting your imaginative self to play here.

The final step is to imagine, "What results could I create by adopting these behaviours and taking these actions?" Again, take your foot off the brake and allow your imagination to run with it. The point of this is to provide you with the opportunity to remove limitations and explore what's possible.

Take a moment to record what you discover about yourself, your mind, your results and your experience of life. Write down the a-ha moments and the nuggets of wisdom that you intend to treasure as a result of your discoveries.

Mindful Mastery

Have you noticed that a lot of success seems accidental? Your mind works on your behalf without you knowing how or why it does. Sometimes, it provides you with exactly what it is you need to achieve success. At other times, it trips you up.

And I'll bet you have been unsure why that happens until now. While it may unsettle you to know your life is the direct result of your programming, the good news is that your life can be intentional and under your control, should you wish to assume responsibility for your machinery. You may not yet know specifically which programme causes you to falter in one area and succeed in another, but at least you know that there is a way to find out, change the programming and realise success in the areas where you've been underperforming.

Mindfulness is a brilliant way for you to discover the contents of your inner world. It is a powerful route to understanding and mastering yourself fully. It opens the door to being in control of who you are and whom you choose to be. It diminishes the experience of being a pawn in life's chess game. You relate to yourself as a whole human being.

Have you ever had the feeling that you have to leave the real you at the door when you enter the workplace or an environment like school? People might invite you to bring your 'full self' to work, for example, but you know this is just a platitude to keep the absentee numbers in check.

The fact is, you already carry your full self with you wherever you go. So, what if you could be OK with your full self wherever you go? What if you knew you were the one in control?

In doing so, you discover more of who you are in the process. Isn't that worth having?

You will not need to dedicate a large chunk of time morning and night to meditate to be mindful. Mindfulness is a practical, in-the-moment form of meditation in which you develop the ability to be present. All it takes is commitment to check in with yourself regularly by focusing on your breath. Before you know it, mindfulness will become automatic.

It can become a habit as natural and obvious as brushing your teeth. You can be a mindfulness master. It can become part of your default settings.

Imagine that.

Making Events and Tasks Mindful

Let's learn how to apply this in your day-to-day experience.

Take out your diary or your task list. If it's morning, look at your day ahead. If it's evening, look at the following day.

As you review the events on the horizon, notice if there is anything that grabs your attention. Perhaps it's a big meeting with an important client. Maybe you have to write a history essay on the French Revolution. It's possible you're scheduled to meet a relative or an old boyfriend for the first time in a long time.

Whatever it is, consider the impact this event is having on you right now.

Here are some questions you could consider when thinking about this forthcoming event or task:

- What do you notice in yourself that calls your attention to this event?
- Describe it as a bodily sensation, a strong emotion, a clear image, an overwhelming impulse or a striking thought.
- What happens in your body as you consider this event?

Remember that what you're dealing with is your default, unconscious reaction to the event. By being mindful, you become conscious of it.

Now, choose one of the mindfulness techniques you've learned and use it to investigate your reaction. You could try a couple if you have time. Notice what arises as you consciously relate to this reaction. Make sure you record what you notice in your journal.

Again, here are some powerful questions that will help you re-engineer your neural pathway and choose a way to respond:

- What do you notice as you bring greater mindfulness and mastery to this issue?
- How does your relationship to this task or event change?
- What becomes available to you as you bring mindfulness to this situation or event?

When you've completed this exercise, look at your diary again and notice what you feel or think about this task or event now. Jot down what you think might help you create the result you most desire. Perhaps there's a deeper level of mindfulness to bring to the situation. If so, see if you can schedule the time to put that into practice.

In the meantime, take a look at other events or tasks in your diary or task list. Has the mindfulness practice shifted your observation or internal conversations about these, too?

A shift in one area can have knock-on effects on others. What you discover is the ability to power your performance with healthy, effective fuel. Think about it this way. Putting water into the engine of a car doesn't make it run faster. In fact, it damages the engine Using the right fuel, whether it's powered by diesel, petrol, electricity or something else, determines whether or not the car runs smoothly and efficiently or not at all.

Take a moment to consider how you might use mindfulness practices in other ways and at other times throughout the day.

Remember our earlier discussion about timesheets? If you have to complete them as part of your daily routine, take a moment to notice how your attitude has changed towards them. If you'd like to improve it, apply the I-AM-I neural pathway re-engineering process to it and see what happens.

By the way, I actively encourage practice and experimentation when it comes to mindfulness. It's all about getting to know yourself and doing what works for you.

How will applying mindfulness practices during your day help you? What processes can you put in place to help remind you to implement mindfulness throughout the day? Being able to put these techniques into practice in the present is the key to this work.

Let's explore another, often hidden area of your life — your thoughts — in the next chapter.

Chapter 11

Examining Your Thoughts

I trust it's becoming clearer and clearer that your thoughts are at the source of everything, including the feelings you have, the bodily sensations you experience, the results you produce in life and the reality in which you live.

This may seem daunting, and you may be of the mindset that it is an impossible task to be responsible for 6,000 thoughts per day.

I'll be honest. You won't be a Jedi Mind Master by the end of the book (and even they make mistakes). However, when you become more mindful of your thoughts, you'll notice something quite interesting. Most of your thoughts are repetitive.

If you think negative thoughts on a repetitive loop, you'll see the world through a mainly negative lens. Other thoughts, while not necessarily deemed 'negative,' may certainly be considered 'limiting'.

Take a look at the types of thoughts you may have at any given moment. Think about them using the context of the definitions provided below, all taken from Oxford Dictionaries. This is not an exhaustive list and the words are listed in alphabetical order rather than in order of importance.

It is a long list of definitions. Bear with me here. As you read the list of definitions, notice what you discover. There is a point to this exercise, but I want you to see what conclusions you come to first. It's the ontological way, remember?

Elevate your awareness by doing a quick mindfulness breathing exercise as you consider each.

Thoughts Defined

Analysis

- Detailed examination of the elements or structure of something
- The process of separating something into its constituent elements

- The identification and measurement of the chemical constituent of a substance or specimen
- The part of mathematics concerned with the theory of function and the use of limits, continuity, and the operations of calculus

Assumption

- A thing that is accepted as true or as certain to happen, without proof
- The action of taking on power or responsibility
- The reception of the Virgin Mary bodily into Heaven
- Arrogance or presumption

Attitude

- A settled way of thinking or feeling about something
- A position of the body indicating a particular mental state
- (Ballet) a position in which one leg is lifted behind with the knee bent at right angles and turned out, and the corresponding arm is raised above the head, the other extended to the side
- (North American) Truculent or uncooperative behaviour
- Individuality and self-confidence
- The orientation of an aircraft or spacecraft, relative to the direction of travel

Belief

- An acceptance that something exists or is true, especially one without proof
- Something one accepts as true or real; a firmly held opinion
- A religious conviction
- Trust, faith or confidence in (someone or something)

Bias

- Inclination or prejudice for or against one person or group, especially in a way considered to be unfair
- A concentration on or interest in one particular area or subject
- A systematic distortion of a statistical result due to a factor not allowed for in its derivation

Choice

- An act of choosing between two or more possibilities
- The right or ability to choose
- A range of possibilities from which one or more may be chosen
- A thing or person which is chosen

Complaint

- A statement that something is unsatisfactory or unacceptable
- A reason for dissatisfaction
- The expression of dissatisfaction
- The plaintiff's reasons for proceeding in a civil court

Concern

- Anxiety; worry
- A cause of anxiety or worry
- A matter of interest or importance to someone
- A complicated or awkward object

Convention

- A way in which something is usually done
- Behaviour that is considered acceptable or polite to most members of a society
- An agreement between states covering particular matters, especially one less formal than a treaty

Daydream

A series of pleasant thoughts that distract one's attention from the present

Decision

- A conclusion or resolution reached after consideration
- The action or process of deciding something or of resolving a question
- The ability or tendency to make decisions quickly; decisiveness

Desire

- A strong feeling of wanting to have something or wishing for something to happen
- Strong sexual feeling or appetite
- Something desired

Explanation

- A statement or account that makes something clear
- A reason or justification given for an action or belief

Fact

- A thing that is known or proved to be true
- Information used as evidence or as part of a report or news article
- Used to refer to a particular situation under discussion
- The truth about events as opposed to interpretation

Fantasy

- The faculty or activity of imagining impossible or improbable things
- A fanciful mental image, typically one on which a person often dwells, and which reflects their conscious or unconscious wishes
- An idea with no basis in reality
- A genre of imaginative fiction involving magic and adventure, especially in a setting other than the real world
- Denoting a competition or league in which participants select imaginary teams from among the players in a real sports league and score points according to the actual performance of their players

Imagination

- The faculty or action of forming new ideas, or images or concepts of external objects not present to the senses
- The ability of the mind to be creative or resourceful
- The part of the mind that imagines things

Interpretation

- The action of explaining the meaning of something
- An explanation or a way of explaining

- A stylistic representation of a creative work or dramatic role

Intuition

- The ability to understand something instinctively, without the need for conscious reasoning
- A thing that one knows or considers likely from instinctive feeling rather than conscious reasoning

Judgement

- The ability to make considered decisions or come to sensible conclusions
- An opinion or conclusion
- A decision of a law court or judge
- A misfortune or calamity viewed as a divine punishment

Justification

- The action of showing something to be right or reasonable
- Good reason for something that exists or has been done
- (Theology) The action of declaring or making righteous in the sight of God
- (Printing) The action or manner of justifying a line of type or piece of text

Logic

- Reasoning conducted or assessed according to strict principles of validity
- A particular system or codification of the principles of proof and inference
- The systematic use of symbolic and mathematical techniques to determine the forms of valid deductive argument
- The quality of being justifiable by reason
- The course of action suggested by or following as a necessary consequence of
- A system or set of principles underlying the arrangements of elements in a computer or electronic device so as to perform a specified task

Memory

- The faculty by which the mind stores and remembers information
- The mind regarded as a store of things remembered
- Something remembered from the past
- The remembering or commemoration of a dead person
- The length of time over which a person or event continues to be remembered
- The part of a computer in which data or program instructions can be stored for retrieval
- A computer's capacity for storing information

Opinion

- A view or judgement formed about something, not necessarily based on fact or knowledge
- The beliefs or views of a group or majority of people
- An estimation of the quality or worth of someone or something
- A statement of advice by an expert on a professional matter
- A barrister's advice on the merits of a case
- A formal statement of reasons for a judgement given

Presumption

- An idea that is taken to be true on the basis of probability
- The acceptance of something as true although it is not known for certain
- An attitude adopted in law or as a matter of policy towards an action or proposal in the absence of acceptable reasons to the contrary
- Behaviour perceived as arrogant, disrespectful, and transgressing the limits of what is permitted or appropriate

Reality

- The state of things as they actually exist, as opposed to an idealistic or notional idea of them
- A thing that is actually experienced or seen, especially when this is unpleasant
- A thing that exists in fact, having previously only existed in one's mind
- The quality of being lifelike
- Relating to reality TV
- The state or quality of having existence or substance
- (Philosophy) Existence that is absolute, self-sufficient or objective, and not subject to human decisions or conventions

Reason

- A cause, explanation, or justification for an action or event
- Good or obvious cause to do something
- (Logic) A premise of an argument in support of a belief, especially a minor premise when given after the conclusion
- The power of the mind to think, understand and form judgements logically
- What is right, practical, or possible; common sense
- One's sanity

Truth

- The quality or state of being true
- That which is true or in accordance with fact or reality
- A fact or belief that is accepted as true.

Unreal Thinking

What did you notice as you reflected on the different types of thought?

What struck me while making this list was how much we rely on thoughts that have no real basis in fact or truth. They are ideas, views, judgements or assumptions, and we believe them to represent truth.

We all rely on modes of thinking that bear no resemblance to reality. It's kind of sobering, isn't it?

We've got a choice; to live in reality or be divorced from it.

And we need to be aware of the illusion that we are making real-world decisions based on reality when we are actually relying on those ideas, views and assumptions to inform our choices.

In looking at the range of thoughts that people have every day, you may have discovered something interesting about yourself and others that leaves you feeling a little disconnected.

I hope it has!

Despite what you believe, our thoughts rarely consist of facts or truth. Most of our thoughts consist of our thoughts *about* a thought or a fact or a piece of evidence or truth, not the fact, evidence or truth itself. And lots of these thoughts about thoughts are unproductive at best, downright destructive at worst.

I was horrified when I discovered this. Why would I (a seemingly intelligent person) give so much time and value to thoughts probably not based on fact, evidence or truth?

I realised I shouldn't be so tough on myself. Even the brightest people on the planet can be guilty of mistaking their thoughts for facts. People ask for your opinion and you are told it is valuable. Sometimes, you are so enamoured with your own thoughts, you create elaborate theories to prove your case, even when it's built on a false premise.

Madness! But it is also something we need to be aware of.

Consider big media companies for a moment.

They are experts in knowing how our minds work even when we don't ourselves. They analyse our behaviour, which has never been easier now that we live out so much of our time on social media. They use this data to influence and manipulate us, personally and collectively.

The motivation? Selling, both things and ideas. The objectivity of the media has been found sorely wanting; it is an information space flooded with misinformation, half-truths and bold-faced lies.

Misinformation's purpose is to communicate stories with the intention of creating a consensus. It used to be known as propaganda. There's often a different, darker agenda lurking underneath, subtly hidden by often emotionally-charged wording.

Misinformation works because most people do not exercise two important thinking functions: critical thinking and discernment. When you exercise critical thinking, you make judgements by analysing *facts*. You develop discernment, or the capacity for keen insight and good judgement, the more you exercise critical thinking.

Without critical thinking and discernment, you are more likely to base decisions on the lowest common denominator in your mental structure, the binary source code of 0s and 1s. When your human brain gives too much weight to the brain's fear reaction, you delude and overwhelm the higher functions of your consciousness machinery with fear-charged thinking in the process.

Put simply, don't believe everything you read, even if the information comes from so-called trusted sources. Exercise all of your mental capacity to make sound judgements. Start by challenging my assertions. Discover the potential of mindfulness for yourself. Be fully human in the process.

Assumption Makes an *A$S* out of *U* and *Me*

It doesn't make sense to invest so much time, energy and effort in pieces of information or points of view that, while fascinating and stimulating, may lead you to a deluded, inaccurate conclusion at best, and a catastrophic consequence at worst. And yet, human beings do it all the time, never stopping to consider the consequences. Arrogance, lazy thinking, bandwagon jumping and hasty, fear-fuelled action can lead you into all sorts of disastrous territories.

Consider that when you began this journey, you may have assumed you knew everything you needed to know about yourself. I hope you've discovered that there's more to you than you realised, and we've only scratched the surface.

For healthy high performance to be a way of life, you have to cultivate a healthy approach to life. Your attitude is key. Keeping an open mind to discovery and possibility, allowing yourself to wonder and exercising curiosity are qualities that will support your success.

However, failing to do that can cause unfortunate, sometimes catastrophic consequences. From a business point of view, a good example of this is Kodak, the US photography and printing company. Despite having invented digital photography, the company failed to acknowledge its disruptive market potential. Believing its reputation would win out, Kodak backed film over digital and lost.

The Kodak management team made a number of strategic decisions that contributed to the company's demise.

What led them to make these decisions? Were they looking at market facts, or were they relying on something else? It could be argued that they failed to read and respond to market trends accurately. Some say the company leadership made arrogant assumptions about their own power in the marketplace. Company failure is certainly a tough but powerful way to learn a lesson that no creature is too big or powerful to meet its demise. [12]

Just ask the dinosaurs.

You may not be in a leadership position. You may not be required to decide your community's direction. That is irrelevant. Believe it or not, every decision you make has a significant impact on the overall performance, whether you are willing to acknowledge it or not.

The same is true in school or sport. Your performance in exams or on the pitch, for example, reflects the overall performance of the school or team and contributes significantly to its standing when compared to other schools or teams. You may not care about your school's position in a league table. You may think that your sporting performance is unimportant in the grand scheme of things. It doesn't stop your performance affecting the school's or the team's overall results.

At some stage in your life, whether it's as a leader in a business or as a parent choosing the right school for your children, you may be in a position that requires you to make that important decision. Having mastery of your thoughts will empower you to make decisions that deliver optimal results.

The decisions you make and the actions you take impact most areas of your life. In fact, if you were to examine it carefully, you would put just about everything you do within some context of performance. You take actions that produce a result, even if it's undesirable.

Knowing yourself to be the source of all results you produce means you have the opportunity to own your contribution to the welfare of your company, your community, your family and your life. Owning your contribution gives you choice that you don't have when you make someone or something else responsible for the results you produce in life.

How might you put this into practice? Choose one event or activity in which you will be engaged today. Describe the event in your journal, and then see if you can identify the types of thought at play as you consider the event.

Refer back to my long list for reminders of the types of thoughts you could be having. If you're really keen, read each type of thought and jot down the thoughts you hear yourself thinking that correspond to that thought category.

Use one or a combination of the breathing exercises to generate a state of mindfulness and then examine your thoughts according to each thought type. Notice what you experience as you complete this exercise, remembering to include other thoughts, emotions, feelings, sensations, impulses, behaviours, actions and results.

As you complete the exercise, you may wish to make new promises about the types of thought you choose to invest in, and the types of thought you choose to set aside, within the context of performance in an area of life.

Take a moment to consider how this change will impact your experience, your behaviours, your actions and ultimately your performance going forward.

Take this discovery with you as we look at how mindfulness makes a difference to your relationships with other people in the next chapter.

Chapter 12

Examining the Quality of Your Relationships

What was it like to become intimately acquainted with the contents of your mind? What does it provide for you that you didn't have before?

- Power?
- Choice?
- Realisation?

In particular, mindfulness paves the way for you to develop an empowered relationship with yourself. After all, the person you are most responsible for in life is YOU!

Mindfulness provides you with the first step to creating a life that you really want and to do it with mastery. If you've made mindfulness part of your regular routine, I hope you have already accelerated your accomplishments and reduced your stress levels.

You've become intimately acquainted with the power of your breath. You've applied mindfulness in your daily routines. You've examined your own realm of experiences with mindfulness. You've altered the experience of tasks and events by applying mindfulness. You've assessed your thoughts. What's next?

People.

Yes, I know. People can be complicated. You've just spent the previous chapters discovering the depths of your own being. Now I'm asking you to deal with other people?

Well, yes, I am, because a key facet of being a brilliant high performer is being able to deal with a wide variety of other people effectively.

Do you need to know a person intimately in order to be able to relate to them? No, you don't. The person you need to know is you. In the process of knowing yourself, you learn a lot about other people.

Here's a little secret. We are all more alike than we care to admit. Though we all have unique experiences and perspectives on life, we also share similar concerns and we all use human neural biological machinery. There may be variations in content and structure, but the basic operation is the same.

Getting to know yourself enables you to know other people, too. It may not have seemed like the obvious way to go about understanding people at the beginning, but I trust you're able to see it for yourself now.

Is that a little more reassuring? I hope so.

The Tangled Webs We Weave

Have you noticed that some people seem to get on with their colleagues, classmates or teammates, while others don't have a clue? Do you assume that people are born with the innate ability to 'get along with others'?

Though there may be some truth in that, relating to others with mastery is a skill that is developed in life. It is a skill that can be learned but it's not one that's usually taught in school or university. This is a shame because smart people are increasingly placing high value on building interpersonal skills. In uncertain times, these opportunities are neglected in favour of developing hard skills deemed 'core' to the success of an organisation, business or academic institution.

I wonder what could be more core to high performance in life than being able to deal with other people? Whether you're running a global organisation or a marathon, you need good people around you to help you accomplish your goals.

Interpersonal skills are essential, and mindfulness can help you elevate yours. Being in control of your responses to others can help you avoid misunderstandings and potential conflict, a welcome result for most people.

Let's examine how mindfulness can help.

Consider how you might approach relationships without mindfulness. A typical reaction is to expect other people and the world to meet your needs. You may even go so far as to demand that others meet your needs. When that doesn't happen, you act out from emotions like disappointment, anger, frustration, powerlessness and resignation.

Does that sound like a healthy way to live?

Co-dependence is the name given to this mindset by professionals like psychologists. It is usually discussed within the context of relationships with strong bonds, such as between romantic partners or other family members. However, in reality, most people are co-dependent with nearly everyone to some extent.

To clarify, this is different from interdependence, which requires a recognition that you're in relationship, your actions impact others, and others' actions impact you.

There's a conscious mutual agreement in place that supports the relationship by being a contribution to it in some way.

One describes a puerile, unconscious way of behaving while the other describes an adult, conscious way of behaving. Any guesses which is which?

What's the point of this discussion? Co-dependent qualities are typically developed in childhood and expressed in adulthood. Interdependence, on the other hand, is characterised by independent, self-sufficient people mutually recognising and honouring the ways in which they interact with each other as part of a wider community.

One is a reaction to something. The other is a response to something. See how this works?

What do you now know having begun the process of applying mindfulness in your life? You can react, or you can respond. When you react, you usually generate the same results you always generate, and these reactions are usually developed at an early stage in your psychological development. If they work for you and others, great. If they don't, you probably want to respond. When you respond, you give yourself the opportunity to explore other avenues. You have the power to promise again and choose an alternative course of action.

You have the power to create different results in your life, and in this case, in your relationships.

How does this work in practice? Consider that you already expect other people to line up with your expectations, opinions, judgements and so on. In the previous chapter, you learned that opinions, judgements and expectations come from subjective thinking. They don't necessarily reflect reality, so giving these thoughts too much consideration is a waste of time and effort.

When others don't fulfil your expectations, you may jump to blame. Sometimes you blame yourself, and sometimes you blame others. Sometimes you blame the system. Sometimes you blame the management team. Sometimes you blame the weather. Guess what? You're in good company! Others do this to themselves and to you, too. It's the nature of the machinery. And it goes round and round in a circle of blame, shame and conflict.

What kind of relationships results from this basis of thought?

Dysfunctional ones, for sure!

Imagine what it would be like if, instead of jumping to conclusions and reacting, you took a minute to check in with your thoughts, images, emotions, bodily sensations, impulses, attitudes, actions, behaviours and results.

Imagine you could merely receive and examine the messages you received without adding or taking anything away.

Doing this allowed you to see things about yourself. You could become aware of how this person's words or actions affect you. Maybe you realised they could 'push your buttons' that create a negative reaction in you.

At that moment, you recognised you could choose a different course of action, that you did not have to remain stuck with an automatic way of being. In taking the risk of trying something new, you created a world of results that was completely unexpected. They may be positive or negative or a bit of both, but they would certainly be unexpected.

What would that be like? What would it open up?

You'd discover that you have choice about how to handle:

- Internal conversations you have with yourself, about yourself
- Internal conversations you have with yourself about other people
- Conversations you have with other people.

Choice in relationships of all types is powerful.

How To Respond in Relationships With Others

When you practise mindfulness in relating to others, you increase your potential to respond in a considered manner. You employ your creative potential to address situations appropriately according to the reality of the situation, rather than operating from a default reactionary position, like a bias or a judgement, that ultimately may or may not be helpful.

Remember those survival-based applications we discussed in an earlier chapter? Think about the fact that while these behavioural patterns seem like default applications, as if they were a part of your intrinsic make-up, they occur this way because they were stored in your memory bank. You forgot where, when and how you created them. Situations similar to the original event activate these patterns of behaviour, sometimes before you even realise this is happening.

How is this possible? The hippocampus, the part of the brain that stores your memories, is much stronger and faster at processing information than the imaginative, problem-solving parts of your brain. When you are confronted with a situation, you will always defer to your memory first to find a strategy that supported your survival in the past. The nervous system, being hardwired for survival of the species, places your safety over creative, critical thinking. [13]

So different aspects of your brain are competing with each other, impeding your creative thinking and decision-making capabilities?! This explains why you often react, rather than respond, to life and within relationships. You are acting out a situation from the past, one that kept you alive. It shows you why you may find yourself in repetitive relationship situations.

What would happen if you could clean out your memory bank of its contents and upgrade the survival strategies to ones that create success in relationships? You would make choices that produce different results. You'd have greater choice about how to respond, and you could experiment to discover what works well and what doesn't.

It's not that your survival strategies are bad or wrong. They may, in fact, be exactly the right way forward in a given situation. Goodness knows, they've kept you alive for this long. The problem is that they can be one-dimensional and limiting, and if you're unconscious of them, you are powerless to change them. Until now, you may have thought it was just a function of your 'personality'. Now you know you have choice. For some of you, that feels exciting. For others of you, it might seem like a burden.

The point is that you would be in control of your thought processes and ultimately your behaviour in a way that you can't be when you leave your choices to your default setting.

Either way, it's your choice. What will you choose?

Why the focus on relationships? Relationships are fundamental to your performance in life. Brilliant relationships, where each person operates from a win-win commitment, produce brilliant environments that deliver brilliant things for the largest number of people.

When you examine the whole world of your thoughts about your relationships in your environment, what does it tell you?

Who Wins?

Start by examining your relationships within the context of two possibilities:

Win-Lose and Win-Win

What's the difference?

Win-Lose thoughts suggest scarcity, which drives competition. Whether the scarcity is real or imagined is irrelevant. It's about the fuel that lies beneath scarcity, which is fear. This scarcity consciousness drives people to act from personal interest, limiting what's possible for themselves and others, which in turn can foster conflict.

Win-Win thoughts, on the other hand, communicate abundance, a recognition that there is enough for everyone.

Again, it's less about whether or not abundance actually exists. It's about the possibilities offered by having an abundance mindset, where gains for everyone are considered and valued. It's an expansive way of viewing the world that fosters creativity and opportunity.

You might believe that you operate from a win-win position already. I assert that if you give thoughts like opinions and judgements more weight in your decision-making than you do thoughts like fact and truth, you are denying others and yourself possibilities not yet visible to you.

The key is to try on a whole host of opinions, judgements, and beliefs without getting stuck with one. Ask yourself what makes your opinion more valid than someone else's. Is it because it's yours?

Of course, it's valid to value an informed opinion from someone with considerable knowledge and skill in a particular area of life. However, it would be a mistake to believe they have all the answers. In fact, 'experts' can get stuck in a paradigm of thinking that disregards other, equally valid realities.

In truth, one opinion is as valid as another. One judgement is as valid as another. One belief is as valid as another. And here's the kicker: none of them is fact.

You believe that your perspective is the most valid. All humans do unless you've made it your mission to master your mind by practising mindfulness. When you look a little deeper, you discover that fear is the fuel that drives you to remain attached to your own point of view as the right one.

The best way to understand this is to put it to the test. Choose a person who provokes a strong reaction in you. It could be a positive or negative reaction.

Take out your journal and answer the following questions:

- Who is this person to you?
- What reaction does he or she provoke?
- What physical, emotional and mental reactions arise as you consider this person?
- What types of thoughts do you notice you're thinking about this person?

Now use one of the mindfulness techniques you've learned as you think about this person. Notice what, if anything, changes when you deepen your conscious awareness of the effect this person creates in you.

What effect does the act of being mindful and the use of the breath have on your thoughts? Your images? Your emotions? Your sensations? Your impulses? Your attitude? Your actions?

Taking the time to breathe through your experience enables you to quieten the fear-based reactive thinking. This gives you the space needed to assess your thoughts, enabling you to respond. Bringing yourself to a state of relaxation switches off the survival instinct, giving you the opportunity to consider different options in your dealings with other people. This is especially beneficial when dealing with someone who pushes your buttons.

Let me give you an example of how this works in practice. A client was struggling to have anything nice to say about his employer. It occurred to him that he was merely a slave doing their bidding. It's not the most empowered place to stand!

When I asked him to breathe, listen to himself and consider the content of his thoughts, he recognised that he was being judgemental and opinionated. His constant complaining prevented him from appreciating the opportunities his employers made available to him and the challenges they faced as business owners.

The first thing he admitted was that his employer reminded him of his father, a figure who could be shouty and overbearing. He was projecting his unresolved feelings about his father, an important past authority figure in his life, onto his employers, the current authority figures in his life.

In searching a little deeper, he realised he was angry about an incident in the past when his employers were not able to meet a request. When he assessed his thoughts with care, he was able to admit that they had valid reasons for rejecting his request. His anger dissipated.

This was coming to the surface as he worried about approaching his employers with another similar request. This time, instead of reacting from the past experience, he chose to respond from a place of empathy for his employer by starting the conversation demonstrating that he understood their challenges as business owners.

What do you think happened? Not only did his employer say yes to his request, but he also acknowledged him for his commitment and hard work by granting him double what he had requested!

At this point, I extend a bonus challenge to you. Put what you've discovered into practice. Create an opportunity to interact with the people in your life and see what happens. Prepare to be amazed. In truth, this is the area where the seemingly impossible happens. When you take ownership of all of yourself and operate with choice and empowerment in your response to life, miracles happen. But, please, don't take my word for it. Go out and discover it for yourself. The next chapter on applying mindfulness to behaviour will provide you with additional insights on how to do just that.

Chapter 13

Applying Mindfulness to Your Behaviour

You have explored the relationship between the mind and the body and the aspect of your experience that bridges the two — the emotions.

Mindfulness lies at the source of mastering your behaviour, which directly correlates to the results you produce.

Let's look at the definition of behaviour. The Cambridge English Dictionary defines behaviour as:

- The way that someone behaves
- The way in which a person, an animal or a substance etc behaves in a particular situation or under particular conditions. [14]

When you read this definition, what do you see? What do you hear? What do you feel?

I see the word 'way' being stated two times. I hear that behaviour exists as an action or set of actions with a distinct flavour, shade or tone (remember our discussion about emotional colour?). I feel that behaviour is descriptive and in being descriptive it reveals something about the person, animal or substance it is describing.

Words like 'erratic', 'odd' and even 'exemplary' often accompany the word behaviour. You can almost experience the behaviour itself without being in its presence, and each of you will have your own version of erratic, odd and exemplary.

It's an interesting word to choose to use in the context of performance. For me, 'behaviour' is automatically loaded with judgement. It begs for a descriptor.

But somehow, because it's used in scientific terms, it's OK to talk about behaviours, which encompass many different facets of experience that I would not class as a 'behaviour'. It's advisable to encourage, even demand, certain 'behaviours' of people, especially in places where people gather to perform a specific function, like business, school and even toddler play groups.

Much has been invested in deploying systems that drive desired behaviours. Are you noticing anything here?

Mindful Performance

So, what is the purpose of being a brilliant performer in life?

As you know by now, I'm not here to give you the answers. I'm here to guide you through the process of discovering the answers for yourself. However, allow me to share my thoughts with you.

Performance could be seen as a behaviour: a conscious set of choices and actions to participate in the environment in which you operate according to the rules agreed by consensus. Sometimes your industry determines the rules. Sometimes your culture determines the rules. Sometimes a management team or committee determines the rules. Sometimes children define the rules. Sometimes politicians define the rules.

Let's look briefly at what a rule is. The Cambridge English Dictionary defines a rule as 'an accepted principle or instruction that states the way things are or should be done, and tells you what you're allowed or not allowed to do'. [15]

Rules enable various moving parts to work together to create a specific goal. In sport, rules enable teams to determine the outcome of a given competition and govern the behaviour of sportspeople. In business, rules provide boundaries for conduct or behaviour that facilitate teamwork, ethical practice and project delivery.

Examples of basic rules in business include the start and end times for working periods and the number of weeks' holiday each person is allowed to take, and so on. In a toddler playgroup, there's usually a defined location, a start and end time, a fee (even if it's just to cover the tea and biscuits) and a code of conduct that parents and children are expected to observe.

Rules serve a useful purpose, namely, to provide a behavioural environment of fair play and clarity about what is and is not expected and acceptable from each person participating in life games that could be called 'work' or 'toddler play group'.

Organisations and communities also have unwritten rules, or codes of behaviour, that might not appear in a contract as an obligation, but it's how things work unofficially.

Let's use the example of particular leaders in a workplace. Do you know what their organisational role is, and do you know how to play according to their rules of engagement?

For instance, one leader, a CFO for example, might place the greatest importance on numbers, financial forecasts and statistics. Think about how your conversation needs to be framed if you want to get buy-in from this person. How will you need to position your idea to boost your chances of this person seeing the value in your presentation?

Another department, perhaps the marketing team, could have a leader who thrives on building creative, emotionally expressive teams. How would you position the same idea to this person to appeal to his or her particular viewpoint and increase your buy-in opportunities? What are the rules by which this person makes decisions?

It's about taking the time to understand the unwritten rules. It requires empathy, or the ability and willingness to walk in another person's shoes for a moment to recognise what's important to them. Demonstrating a willingness to at least consider a situation from another person's point of view builds bridges that can help you expand your performance in life.

You have strengths and weaknesses, like everyone else. You have a set of well-developed skills, and you may be lacking skills in another area. Does this mean you are limited to relying upon operating in one way for the rest of your life?

Not at all!

Key skills that you and every high performer need to develop are the ability to read people and situations accurately and the ability to understand how to meet people and situations where they are, not from where you are.

This means that, after assessing your own position or situation, you take yourself out of that position or situation and put yourself in the shoes of the other person or situation.

You've been learning how to direct your attention inwards to affect transformation within yourself. Now it's time to direct your attention outwards to create results in an external environment. How might you do this?

Active listening and empathy are key skills that you develop through the practice of mindfulness. When you are able to observe, hear and empathise with yourself with a degree of acuity, you can apply the same principles to others.

Imagine yourself in conversation with a leader in your community. What do you notice? What thoughts arise? What emotions arise? What physical sensations do you notice? Is it almost immediate, as if a 'default setting' has been triggered?

Now take a moment to apply one of the mindfulness techniques you learned in the first part of the book and notice what occurs. What happens to the thoughts, emotions and physical sensations? How does your attitude change?

How might your actions and behaviour change as a result? What is left?

When you bring awareness to what you are really thinking and experiencing, you can acknowledge your thinking, explore it in more depth and engage with it. You can ask yourself if your thoughts will produce the result you want. If your thoughts produce an unwanted, unproductive emotional or physical reaction, you have the opportunity to assess them and change them.

Notice how the content of your original conversation changes about the leader. Are you able to see things you weren't able to see before? What difference will that make to your relationship with this person?

Though most thoughts, emotions and sensations are fleeting, some just keep recurring, no matter what you do. Sometimes it seems as though you are on a hamster wheel going round and round in circles.

When you become mindful of the recurring thought that generates recurring emotional and physical reactions, you can change it.

It helps to apply the I-AM-I process to recurring thoughts, starting with a result and reverse-engineering the experience to the original thought, which you can then change and create new, more productive neural pathways. Review the chapter to remind yourself of the process, and of course, get in touch if you want to be guided through it. I'll tell you more about how you can do that towards the end of the book.

With more entrenched thoughts, it makes a massive difference to seek the support of someone who is trained as a coach or therapist, who can see what you can't see. The important thing is that you are committed to owning your own mastery.

The truth is, you already are master of your own mind. It may not feel like it and yes, it takes practice and discovery to believe it. Mastery requires it. Is it worth the effort? I hope I've shown you that it definitely is. The opportunity now is to step into it and own it.

Pivoting

I'll share a quick way to change your thoughts in a moment through an exercise called pivoting. Here's how it works.

Imagine you have a big meeting coming up with a formidable character. It could be a company leader, the head of the school orchestra or your local MP. Listen to the thoughts going round in your head. They can range from something like, 'I cannot screw this up,' to 'What if he doesn't like me?' to 'I'm not good enough to do this.'

Take each thought in turn and pivot it towards something that is less aligned with a negative outcome and more aligned with a neutral or positive outcome. Take, for example, the thought, 'I cannot screw this up.' How might you pivot this thought towards something that can actually support your success in the meeting?

You start by asking yourself questions like:

- What makes me think I'll screw it up?
- What would screwing it up look like?
- What's the worst that can happen if I screw it up?
- What's the best that can happen if I screw it up?
- What could I do now to prevent screwing it up?
- What if I don't screw it up?
- What if I achieve success?
- What would success look like?
- What would I have to think to make success happen?
- What actions would I need to take to make success happen?
- What do I choose?

What comes out of having pivoted your thinking to challenge the narrative 'screw it up'? You might examine a situation where you did 'screw it up' to understand what didn't work so well at that moment. You might think it prudent to do some research on the person you're meeting so you enter the meeting feeling prepared. You might spend some time making a list of points you want to address.

Suddenly, a situation that seemed pretty scary now becomes more doable, all because you've done the thinking around it to address a nagging concern.

You are empowered to create success intentionally when you become responsible for your thoughts and apply mindfulness to integrate your thoughts, emotions and behaviours towards accomplishing a specific result. The first step in being responsible for your thoughts is to know what you're thinking.

How do you accomplish that? By applying mindfulness, naturally.

You have been exploring different routes to access the contents of your mind. The magic lies partly in knowing how to apply the techniques and partly in recognising the doors that will open for you when you apply them.

You know what? I think you're nearly ready to walk through those doors on your own. Don't you?

Now, we are nearing the end of the book. Before we go, I want to introduce you to a very important part of your mind. We've spent a lot of this book actively developing it. Let's meet it face to face.

Chapter 14

Meeting the Witness

Being a Brilliant High Performer

As a high performer, you naturally want to produce the best results possible. It's the very essence of the high performance mindset.

You want to do this for a number of reasons that may include:

- Expanded opportunities
- Status
- Profitability
- Fulfilment
- Promotion or ranking
- Salary increase
- Challenge
- Satisfaction.

You probably already produce brilliant results. Do you acknowledge yourself for it? Do you regularly take the time to recognise your accomplishments?

Think about how you produce brilliant results. If you applied the I-AM-I model you learned a few chapters ago and take a result back to the original thought, what would you find?

If I had asked you that question at the beginning of our time together, chances are you would have stared at the page wondering where the heck to begin. If you've been putting these techniques into practice regularly, you're probably pretty comfortable with the exercise, and you might even be able to tell me the answer after a few moments spent breathing and reflecting and noticing.

Equally, there will be areas where you recognise you are not performing as well as you would like. If you applied the I-AM-I model to the results you are producing in this area, taking the result back to its source, the thought, what would you find?

Many factors contribute to a result, especially in an environment where there are several people involved in accomplishing the result. Because of this, it's tempting to look for the fault outside yourself.

While you cannot be responsible for everything that happens, you can be responsible for your contribution to the result delivered. It might seem on the surface that the responsibility does not lie at your feet. Consider that every person involved is, at some level, responsible for the outcome.

Mindfulness and Accountability

President Eisenhower famously placed a placard on his desk that said, 'The buck stops here.' Some people branded him a megalomaniac. I see it as his reminder to remain accountable for his actions and for the actions of everyone who served the American people under his presidency.

How accountable are you for your actions? How accountable are you for the results you produce? How do your levels of accountability differ when considering successes versus failures?

Accountability is one of those words that frightens people. It causes you to put yourself on the line for something by making a commitment and evaluating how well you delivered on that commitment. But is it really scary, or is it another one of those fear-based survival thoughts that is limiting you?

I don't think I need to answer that question for you. You already know the answer.

If you'd like to produce more results on the success side and fewer on the failure side, it's worth getting to the source of your contribution to both. Being accountable for the results you produce, regardless of whether you'd consider them successes or failures, is critical. This applies to both intrinsic results, like your emotional state, as well as extrinsic results like landing a new client, meeting an essay deadline or consistently breaking par.

At the beginning of the book, we looked at how people typically determine their level of performance by measuring results in reality. I've guided you to explore what internal processes are involved that affect your performance.

While some people love data and measure everything, some people hate it and avoid it like the plague. Still, other people don't understand data's value enough to even give it a second thought. See if you can remember what you thought and how you felt when we discussed performance measures like grades and KPIs. Notice what you are experiencing right now, and see if anything has changed. Record what you discover in your journal.

This is what self-mastery is all about. It is about recognising that your thoughts are at the source of everything about you, including your emotions, physical sensations, impulses, actions, behaviours and ultimately results. If you want to produce amazing results, you must think the thoughts that generate the environment to bring those results into being.

Reread the definition of behaviour. What do you notice about the definition? What immediately jumps out at me is that behaviour is used to describe human beings, animals, inanimate objects like computers and natural phenomena, like hurricanes.

Where's the humanity in that? It brings me full circle, back to one of my introductory points, that in life, human beings are increasingly objectified and equated to a number or an object like a computer, a creature or a desk.

Is that what makes a human life brilliant, equating the very community that creates the results and causes its success to a series of numbers, an insect or a lump of metal? Does it make sense for you, one of life's high performers, to regard yourself as a machine?

Everyone clearly has choice, but my answer would be a firm no. You are much more than that.

Meeting and Mastering the Real YOU

Now, I realise I've used the word 'machinery' to refer to your body.

Guess what? You are not your body. You use your body to experience life, but you are not your body. When I asked you to observe your thoughts, images, emotions, sensations, impulses, attitudes and actions, who was doing the observing?

YOU!

Say hello to an essential part of you, the Witness, the you that's with you all the time; there at a moment's notice to help you be the big, bold, beautiful, brilliant person you really are.

It is the Witness, not the machine thinking the thoughts, that helps you see the fullness of you. This is what I've been guiding you to recognise and apply. I have been coaching you to build the muscle of activating the Witness at a moment's notice to provide you with the power of conscious observation.

Activating the Witness could be classed as a behaviour, in the sense that it is a response to an event or a stimulus, but it's a special behaviour. What makes it special? It is distinctly human.

You've probably seen people assert mastery of something. You are a master at certain skills in your life already, and you know that when you take responsibility and commit to something, you can make anything happen.

I'm inviting you to be master of YOU.

As you have learned, it begins in the mind. If you can conceive it, you can achieve it, so the saying goes. Your mind can create marvellous ideas and possibilities. It can also create needless barriers that thwart your progress.

The good news is this. You get to choose which thoughts you support and which ones you discard. Really, you do. Thoughts come and go. You have the power to choose which ones you follow and which ones you release.

Now, I want to challenge something I put forth a few sessions ago, and that is the notion that you are your thoughts. Allow me to rephrase that. You are not your thoughts. You are the part that observes the thoughts.

You are the Witness. It's the part of you that observes without attachment. In meditative, contemplative or prayerful paths, activating the Witness enables the practitioner to begin the process of achieving what some call enlightenment and others call wisdom.

What Does This Mean?

But what do enlightenment and wisdom mean? You know how I love definitions, so here goes.

The Cambridge English Dictionary defines enlightenment as:

- The state of understanding something
- The period in 18th Century Europe when many people began to emphasise the importance of science and reason, rather than religion and tradition. [16]

Is enlightenment the point of mindfulness? In fact, it is one of them. In activating the Witness and keenly observing yourself, you are shedding light on aspects of yourself that previously had remained unknown to you. You were 'in the dark' about it.

Not anymore. By applying mindfulness, you are able to understand yourself.

That's pretty useful!

Now let's do the same for wisdom.

The Cambridge English Dictionary defines wisdom as:

- The ability to use knowledge and experience to make good decisions and judgements. [17]

What's the difference between enlightenment and wisdom?

Enlightenment is a state of understanding. Wisdom is the ability or skill to utilise understanding. You could see it as the ability to actively apply enlightenment to your life. One is a receptive experience, like breathing in. The other is an active experience, like breathing out.

At this point, allow me to clear up a little confusion about enlightenment. In certain circles, it is believed that you attain a level of consciousness at which all suffering ends.

In reality, enlightenment does not work this way. You certainly reach significant milestones in your mindfulness journey, where it feels as though you make a quantum leap in discovering the nature of reality. What lies around the corner is another aspect of reality you haven't considered.

Enlightenment is a process of unfolding, of continuing to shed light on aspects of reality that once lay just beyond your grasp. When you reach that layer, you discover there's another layer and another layer and another layer. The layers go on for eternity.

It takes wisdom, or the application of enlightenment, to come to this conclusion and be content with it.

It's up to you to choose just how far into the realms of consciousness you venture. You can spend a lifetime searching and never find the end.

Because there is no end. Life and its wonders are eternal. Just look at yourself in relationship to the environment we call the Universe. We're a minute speck in a realm of experience so vast, we can't even begin to truly understand what this vastness means.

Now, in the beginning, you may not have been present to the possibility of knowing yourself as intimately as you do now. You are hopefully more enlightened and wise than you were when you began this journey. What made that possible is your activation of the Witness in your consciousness by practising mindfulness.

Mindfulness allows you to come into contact with this part of yourself, an aspect of being human that, once developed, will assist you to make wise decisions. Rather than being constantly thrown about by the storms of life, you can lift yourself out of the water to assess the situation from a bird's eye view. This gives you choice that you can't see when you're swirling around in the chaos.

You claim the power to move life rather than having life move you. This mastery is the true source of your power and your ability to scale great heights as a high performer.

Mindfulness opens the door to a whole new realm of knowing yourself. It's the first step on your journey to self-mastery.

Mindfulness Breeds Wisdom

One of the reasons I developed my mindfulness courses for high performers was the realisation that, in leading people through my more advanced leadership development course, there was something missing in students' ability to listen to and actively hear themselves think on a deeper level.

The world is so focused on producing results in the external world that it disregards what's happening on the inside. This, as I see it, is a failing of education in general. Things are changing, albeit slowly. Emotional welfare sits on the agenda in many schools, higher educational establishments and businesses in principle, if not always in practice.

Socrates is credited with saying, 'To know thyself is the beginning of wisdom.' Mindfulness provides a powerful yet simple route to you taking your first step on the path to wisdom.

However, wisdom is not a passive quality. Just look at the definition. It's active in discernment and decision-making. It's a quality based on both knowledge and experience. Remember me telling you how valuable a teacher's experience is? It helps you develop wisdom, a priceless gift to treasure.

Getting to know yourself lets you get to know others on a deeper level. This will be of significant benefit to you in life.

In setting off on this voyage of discovery, you begin to see reality for what it really is, and not what you think, imagine, feel or sense it is. Truth builds a strong core for healthy high performance in life.

A way to embrace the gifts of self-knowledge and its accompanying wisdom is to acknowledge what you have already accomplished. Acknowledgement enables you to distinguish and own your accomplishments and the lessons you learned along the way.

So, as we come to the end of our journey, I'd like you to take a moment to review your progress over the course of reading this book and appreciate the progress you've made.

I would like to acknowledge you for being the kind of person who has put these techniques into practice. It takes courage to enter into an unknown realm, the depths of your own being, in service to being a responsible, productive person willing to be a contribution to others. Keep being the amazing person that you are and keep practising mindfulness. You've only scratched the surface of discovering just how deep your brilliance goes.

Appreciate the Witness, the part of you that is always present and always willing to help you bring light to the dark places. I actively encourage you to check in as often as you can, and I'd like to leave you with a very special mindfulness exercise that you can perform at any time. It is designed to get you in touch with the very essence of you.

You Are Valuable

Set your timer for 10 minutes. Take yourself through the complete body mindfulness exercise to enter into a fully relaxed state.

When you have completed the mindfulness exercise, bring your attention to the point between your eyebrows. On the in breath, repeat to yourself: 'I am valuable.' On the out breath, repeat to yourself: 'I have value.' Repeat the full affirmation seven times.

Bring your attention to your heart centre. On the in breath, repeat to yourself: 'I am valuable.' On the out breath, repeat to yourself: 'I have value.' Repeat the full affirmation seven times.

Bring your attention to the space below your navel. On the in breath, repeat to yourself: 'I am valuable.' On the out breath, repeat to yourself: 'I have value.' Repeat the full affirmation seven times.

Allow your attention to encompass your entire body from head to toe. On the in breath, repeat to yourself: 'I am valuable.' On the out breath, repeat to yourself: I have value." Repeat the full affirmation until the time is up.

When the timer sounds, allow yourself to come to a natural stop in repeating the phrase and sit in the experience for a moment. Notice what's present for you as you allow your entire nervous system to align itself to the essential truth that you have value, that you are valuable, that you are a valuable person, that you are here to be of value to others, and to yourself, and that you create value as a high-performing member of the human community.

As we reach the end of this journey to self-knowledge and self-mastery, I want to extend a final invitation to you. I request that you create a pledge to yourself to live from the truth that you are important. You matter. Regard and respect all of you.

I encourage you to keep activating the Witness and let mindfulness pave the way to your expression of performance brilliance in all its fullness. There's so much of you still waiting to be discovered by YOU.

You are valuable. You are brilliant.

Now that you know it, go and live it. I'm rooting for you.

Chapter 15

What's Next?

What have you discovered for yourself in taking this stroll through the streets of mindfulness?

I hope you've discovered that:

- It's easier than you think to apply
- It makes a difference in unexpected ways to your ability to perform in life
- It helps you improve your performance with a reduced amount of effort
- It encourages you to breathe out AND in (and out and in and…).

The ultimate goal of mindfulness is that it allows you to fully enter the flow with life, bringing new-found ease to your daily routine.

Most of us spend a lot of time performing repeated tasks. It makes a difference to our health and our happiness to approach the challenges of life with a sense of rhythm, flow and completeness. Remembering to use these times as opportunities to apply mindfulness to your life enables you to make it a natural part of your everyday existence.

Imagine what your workplace, school, sports team, home or community could be like if you all approached your roles from a mindful perspective.

The idea of healthy high performance would stop being an ideal and become reality.

If you've found this of value, I invite you to keep practising. I invite you to share what you've learned with colleagues, students, family and friends, and share the love by leaving a review. This book may have generated more questions than answers. Maybe you'd like to work with me. If so, get in touch.

Finally, keep your eyes peeled for my second book, in which I'll be guiding you to bring a deeper level of mindfulness to relationships.

In the meantime, keep practising mindfulness and uncovering the genuine source of your brilliance. It's already there waiting for you to find it. As you breathe both out and in, just notice. That's all there is to do.

Endnotes

1. https://breathworkonline.com/contraindications/
2. https://dictionary.cambridge.org/dictionary/english/performance
3. https://www.etymonline.com/word/performance
4. https://www.lexico.com/en/definition/dissociation
5. For more information on this topic, I highly recommend The Secret Life of the Unborn Child: How You Can Prepare Your Baby for a Happy, Healthy Life, by Dr. Thomas Verny and John Kelly, published 1982 by Penguin Random House. It's a classic!
6. https://www.etymonline.com/word/reaction
7. https://www.etymonline.com/word/respond
8. https://dictionary.cambridge.org/dictionary/english/pledge
9. For more information on the body's wisdom and capacity to heal trauma, I highly recommend reading Waking the Tiger: Healing Trauma - The Innate Capacity to Transform Overwhelming Experiences, by Peter A. Levine, Ann Frederick and Chris Sorensen, 1997, North Atlantic Books.
10. For a simplified introduction to Adler's work, I recommend The Courage to Be Disliked: How to Free

Yourself, Change Your Life and Achieve Real Happiness, by Ichiro Kishimi and Fumitake Koga, published 2018 by Allen and Unwin Books.

11. https://wileypsychologyupdates.com/psychology-update/psychology-update-humans-have-more-than-6000-thoughts-per-day-psychologists-discover/

12. https://www.forbes.com/sites/chunkamui/2012/01/18/how-kodak-failed/#5993f1d46f27

13. For a simple but engaging explanation of the brain's basic processing functionality, check out The Chimp Paradox: The Acclaimed Mind Management Programme to Help You Achieve Success, Confidence and Happiness by Professor Steve Peters, published 2012 by Vermilion.

14. https://dictionary.cambridge.org/dictionary/english/behaviour

15. https://dictionary.cambridge.org/dictionary/english/rule

16. https://dictionary.cambridge.org/dictionary/english/enlightenment

17. https://dictionary.cambridge.org/dictionary/english/wisdom

About L A Worley

L A Worley, author of *The Healthy High Performance Way*, has been opening doors to opportunities her entire career.

She started her career by launching Silicon Valley start-up technology companies in Europe during the dot com boom. Loving people development, she went on to help people recover from a variety of mental health challenges as a psychotherapist and coach.

She enables people to create lives they love, coaching them to mindfully listen, learn and lead, building self-worth and confidence in the process. She loves guiding people to discover how to create a life filled with power, freedom and fulfilment.

When she's not saving the world, she likes to sing, dance, discover new restaurants, drink fine wine, ski and trek in the British countryside.

To facilitate your performance elevation, L A Worley has created **The Healthy High Performance Workbook**, a journal that accompanies this book, and **90-Day Healthy High Performance Planner**, a daily pivot planner. Both tools help you actively upgrade your high performance mindset and accomplish your SMARTER goals.

For data lovers, she has created the Healthy High Performance Tracker, an online tool that will help you track the shifts in your intrinsic and extrinsic motivations and the impact this has on your performance. Download it here: https://businessbrilliance.co.uk/performance-tracker/

As well as working with clients on a one-to-one basis, L A Worley creates bespoke programmes that help people apply her I-AM-I methodology to performance, relationships and leadership.

For more information on how you can access these tools and take your performance to great heights with L A Worley's help, please visit https://businessbrilliance.co.uk/.

Here's to healthy high performance — and your success!